Heaven's helper

"MY LITTLE STAR"

A woman in daily communication with
Heaven helping those in need

MAUREEN CAPISTRAN

ISBN: 978-0-692-89175-9 (Paperback)
Copyright © 2017 by Maureen Capistran
HOLY Heart Publishing
Contact email: maureencapistran@aol.com

Please feel free to email me your prayer requests and I will pray for your
intentions.
I am not able to answer any personal questions due to the high volume
of mail I receive.

Covers and interior design
Have **O**ur **L**ord in **Y**our **Heart Ministry**
Cover/Interior Art: Shutterstock.com

*"A good player stays focused on the ball,
the ball being my Son, Jesus."*

Blessed Virgin Mary to Maureen
February 16, 2001

Acknowledgements

I would like to thank all those who believed in me and my story and helped make this book a reality. In their humility they have chosen to remain anonymous. I am forever indebted to all the holy priests who tirelessly helped and guided me along my spiritual journey. I pledge my eternal love, gratitude and service to God the Father, Jesus Christ, The Holy Spirit, our Blessed Mother and St. Michael the Archangel.

CONTENTS

Rev. Aniello Salicone, SX
Xaverian Missionary Fathers

November 26, 2014

To Whom It May Concern,

I, Father Aniello Salicone of the Xaverian Missionary Fathers, can testify this about Maureen Capistran. I met Maureen in 1998 in Massachusetts. When she came to me, not knowing she had been chosen by God, she was experiencing demonic attack. Being a workaholic in the secular world she was unaware of any type of manifestation regarding spiritual activity, good or bad.

I told her to pray my favorite prayer: "Thank you Jesus for loving me as your number One. Please, help me to love You, others and myself the way you love me.", and I told her not to be afraid. She obeyed, and she was happy to see the evil defeated. I told her that she was going to be able to talk to Jesus. So, it happened. She was greatly helped to overcome the evil one, by the words and encouragement of Jesus, and later on Mary and Saint Michael.

She was told that she was going to be helping people. But she didn't know in which way yet. I asked her to join me when I was invited to pray with sick people, and at healing services. She learned from me and was very devoted to the sick. She then started receiving the gift of knowledge. She was told by Heaven the problem or sickness of the person for whom we were praying and many times she was told the way to treat or solve the problems. I helped her to discern whether what she heard was through her gift from God or from the evil one.

I saw that the Lord was guiding her in growing in her spiritual life. I became her Spiritual Director, and she always contacted me (and continues to do so) with questions as she evolved along her spiritual journey. I have seen enormous progress she has made in the last few years. The necessity of prayer, the reality of Heaven, Hell and Purgatory, the generosity in helping others have a deep root within her! She has learned to offer her suffering to Jesus and Mary for her salvation and others. She has the gift of knowledge and also the gift of healing. She knows that the Healer is God, and she has gratefully accepted the role of His humble instrument.

I am confident that through her gifts she can be of great help to people she meets now and in the future.

In faith,
Rev. Aniello Salicone

Rev. Laurence V. Brault
Diocesan Priest

March 20, 2020

My Dear Friends,

My name is Fr. Laurence Brault and I am pastor of St. Gabriel the Archangel parish in Upton, Massachusetts – a parish in the Diocese of Worcester. For the past eight years we have been conducting a monthly healing service calling upon the intercession of St. Raphael the Archangel and using the St. Raphael Oil, a sacramental that is prepared by the Archangel St. Raphael Holy Healing Ministry. Over these years I have come to know Maureen Capistran and have been blessed to see, first hand, the powerful spiritual gifts that God has allowed to be manifested through her. As a recipient of messages from Jesus, Mother Mary and the Archangel Michael she has guided people to open their hearts to God's healing love. Over the past two years, I have responded personally to a call to be a vehicle of healing for many who have come to me. Maureen has been at my side helping me to focus my prayer on the specific concerns that weigh down these people. She has been a beacon of hope and promise for so many. At the same time, she exercises these gifts humbly and at all times through the direction she receives from above. Her spiritual messages, also received through the direction of Jesus, Mother Mary, and the Archangel Michael has lifted up the hearts of all who have heard these messages. I can attest to the credibility of these gifts and pray that they will continue to be of assistance to the people of God. Yours in Christ,

Rev. Laurence V. Brault

Rev. Joseph F. Whalen, M.S.*
Missionary Priests of La Salette

September 29, 2014

My Dear Friends,

I have known Maureen since May of 2007. She has been a great asset to my Healing Ministry. She has sat with many people, is very honest, humble and has an excellent rapport with people of all ages. Her communication skills are excellent. She has been blessed with true mystical gifts from Almighty God. By exercising these gifts she has helped numerous people of all ages return to God. She is a Roman Catholic in good standing, obedient and faithful to the teachings of Sacred Tradition, Sacred Scripture, and the Magisterium.

In Christ Jesus,
Rev. Joseph F. Whalen, M.S.

*Fr. Joseph Whalen went to his eternal rest in 2016.

Rev. John E. Welch, M.S.
Missionary Priests of La Salette

September 19, 2014

To Whom It May Concern,

I have known Maureen for five years, four of which I have been her Spiritual Director. I can attest to the fact that she has many gifts from God. She has used them well with permission of priests and her former Spiritual Director. Using her gift of knowledge she has directed psychologists who assist deliverance priests. She has also attended many deliverances with priests who specialize in this area and have specifically requested her assistance. She has helped many people renew their faith, and has an inner strength that could only come from the Holy Spirit working within her. Maureen does not look upon her gifts as a means to her own personal sanctification. She recognizes that they have been given to her for building up of the body of Christ on this earth. At present she is doing healing work, as her Spiritual Director I have no doubt as to her ability in this area.

Yours respectfully in Christ,
Rev. John E. Welch, M.S.

Rev. Paul Desmarais
Diocesan Priest

May 27, 2015

To Whom It May Concern,

I am pleased to write this letter on behalf of Maureen Capistran. I have known and worked with Maureen for several years. I am a diocesan priest and pastor, and also the Director of Deliverance ministry for my diocese. I have invited Maureen to accompany me on many deliverance cases. She has been exceptional in her assistance and contribution. Her work with me has consistently reflected a deep level of insightfulness and wisdom. She has the gift of healing, knowledge, and discernment. Because of her deep humility she is able to complete any task with great discernment, wisdom and prudence. She has a very deep spirituality and a very intimate love for Jesus Christ and Our Lady. She has helped many people understand their problems and return to God. Maureen's life is one of service and love for all people. Should you require any additional information regarding Maureen, please feel free to contact me.

Sincerely Yours in Christ,
Rev. Paul Desmarais

INTRODUCTION

This is a true story. Some names and identifying details have been changed to protect the privacy of certain individuals.

I was an ordinary person with little education, who had great motivation and determination to work and succeed in the material world. I worked hard. I persevered. I became successful in the area of real estate through my fortitude and persistence. And then, completely unaware, I was chosen by God. As I later learned, the purpose was to show that He does exist and that He has an infinite, unconditional love for each and every one of us. However, I would first have to endure seven years of demonic attack without a lifeline from Heaven. This was followed by a physical and spiritual healing from Jesus. I then underwent three years of training with Jesus, the Blessed Mother and St. Michael the Archangel. After my spiritual formation I was given beautiful gifts by God the Father to help others. I was finally working for God and with one of His angels, St. Michael the Archangel, to help those in need. I see and hear Jesus and I hear the Blessed Mother and St. Michael. I communicate through thought with them. This being, I pray and call for them silently. Then I hear them *audibly* respond by speaking into my right ear. Jesus assigned St. Michael to direct and guide me on my mission here on earth. I also receive visions and dreams to assist in God's work. I've learned that when one is called by God for a specific mission, He always provides the grace to complete it. The gifts God has given me are not for myself, but to help others. I am in the service of God's will. I am just one little piece of God's puzzle. My purpose here on earth is to direct the focus on God, not myself and to help others.

I have always had a holy priest beside me since the onset of my gift. My first spiritual director was a very gifted Xaverian priest, Fr. Aniello Salicone. After he was transferred to Chicago, I was led to Fr. Joe Whalen, the LaSalette missionary healing priest. While working with Fr. Whalen's ministry, I met Fr. John E. Welch, also a LaSalette missionary priest. He became my next spiritual director about the time he was celebrating his fiftieth anniversary of ordination in 2010.

I have never asked for money for the work that I do. I received these gifts freely from God and these gifts should be given freely to help whoever God sends to me. The fruits of this ministry have been many and the miracles countless. I am continually in awe of God's infinite power. Fr. Aniello, my first spiritual director, told me to keep a journal because one day my experiences and the messages I received would become a book. Later on, I prayed to Jesus and the Blessed Mother and asked if this book was their will. Jesus said, "Book of treasures, I am drawing light as the presence of day." Another time, I had been praying to St. Michael and asking him if it was God's will for me to get this book written. His reply, "Whatever makes Our Father happy will be." After putting all my experiences on tape, I prayed to St. Michael and asked what the title of the book should be. "My Little Star, (as he calls me) that is the easy part, 'My Little Star'! This will be the title."

When I asked St. Michael what the purpose of this book was, he told me, "Through the teachings Heaven bestowed on you, people will know that God exists, how Jesus loves each and every one of us, discernment, and that God's powers are different than man's powers, Heaven's gentleness and the power of one."

God does exist and he is involved personally with all of us. I pray that this book finds its way into the hands of all people, from all races, religions and nationalities. The most important message from this book is not about me, nor the gifts and knowledge God has so freely given me to help others. The message is for the reader to come to know who God truly is and how much he loves us and what God can do for the purpose and salvation of all. God is love, and if we live in love, then we live in God. May God Bless you all abundantly through His Infinite Love,

Maureen

PROLOGUE

In June of 2013, Maureen saved my life. For centuries God has gifted ordinary men and women with exceptional gifts and charisms to build up His church. Maureen is one of these people. I met her at a healing service in May of 2007 and soon began to witness her astounding gifts. Having met many people who claimed to have mystical gifts, but actually didn't, I was very skeptical and didn't have much interest. But I got to know her more and more and came to see that her gifts were indeed real. My barometer was simply this: she always had a solid Roman Catholic priest as a Spiritual Director; she never asked for money when helping someone; and there were countless fruits coming from her work. She was so humble and never even spoke of her gift: none of this was for herself, she exercised her gifts to build up the body of Christ. In a nutshell, she sees and hears Jesus, and hears the Blessed Mother and St. Michael. Heaven trained her for many years. The purpose? She has been chosen to help bring souls back to God. I've personally witnessed many miracles, but it is my objective here to tell you of my own miracle and give my own awe-inspiring account of a profound encounter with one of Heaven's angels.

In June of 2013, Maureen and I were having coffee and she "saw" a tumor in my right breast. Not wanting me to panic, she asked if I had had a mammogram lately. I said "Not for a few years," and I quickly changed the subject. I was afraid, because I knew if she mentioned it, there was a good reason. Later that day her angel urged her to tell me again, which she did. This time, I listened. I was very anxious about the whole thing, but the angel reassured Maureen that I would be alright.

I went to the doctor for a mammogram. Several days later I received a letter saying there was an anomaly in my right breast and that another mammogram was required. I went in for a second mammogram and this time they ordered an ultrasound to define more clearly the spot they were seeing. After the ultrasound, the doctor told me that the edges were suspiciously irregular. Then a biopsy was scheduled. I was very distressed at this point, and asked Maureen to pray to the angel for some guidance. She never wavered. She repeated what he said... all would be OK, not to worry, that I would survive this.

On August 1, I was on my way to Boston's Logan airport to fly to a Catholic conference with two priests I served. My cell phone rang, and it was a nurse from the hospital. She confirmed she was speaking to me, and then regretfully informed me that the biopsy came back positive for cancer.(I had asked them previously to inform me by telephone as I traveled so extensively) My heart sank, but I vowed to make the best of the weekend, which I did. When I returned from the conference I was with Maureen again and another nurse called me for a standard medical interview. After the medical interview she asked "Why did you have the mammogram at this time?" I said, "Do you want to hear the truth?" and she said "Yes." I then related this story to her. She said, "I do believe you, as we see many miracles at the hospital."

She then went on to tell me that I had to choose a surgeon for removal of the tumor. Before the nurse could read the doctor's names, Maureen closed her eyes and heard the angel say, "Ed, Ed, Ed," the angel had already chosen "Dr. Ed." Before she could read the list of surgeons, I told her I wanted Dr. Ed. The nurse was astounded, I told her she did not have to read the other surgeon's names, that Dr. Ed was the one I was choosing. She asked how I knew there was a Dr. Ed and why I selected him. I told her I didn't know there was a Dr. Ed, that the angel had just chosen him! At this point she was speechless and the phone went dead; when she regained her composure she told me that Dr. Ed was a very holy Christian man and a wonderful surgeon. She felt he would be a perfect match for me. Shortly thereafter I met with Dr. Ed and I found him to be just that.

On August 23, I had the lump removed (the size of a small pea) and some lymph nodes tested. Before the surgery Dr. Ed came into the preoperative area and took my hand. He got down on his knees and prayed to Jesus for a successful surgery, he prayed to the Holy Spirit that He would anoint and guide his hands so he would get all the cancer. I was so grateful that God was watching over me and that Maureen's angel had guided me to this wonderful surgeon. My surgery was in the morning. By noon, I was home, feeling completely normal. I made a cup of coffee and went to work on my computer. I recuperated well, had very little pain and everything healed fine.

On Thursday August 29th, I received a call from Dr. Ed. He told me he successfully removed all the margins and that the lymph nodes were cancer free, just as the angel said! I have a minimal scar, with no disfigurement at all. It has been 5 years and I am "OK," no sign of cancer. The nurses gave my case the classification "ADT" which they said means, "Angel Detected Tumor." So on that morning in June of 2013, God saved my physical life through His instrument Maureen Capistran and her angel St.Michael. When God performs a miracle it's most often for the benefit of more than one person or one purpose. Had I not had a strong faith in God, believed in her gift and the angel, I never would have followed through with a mammogram and most likely not be here to give witness to God's infinite mercy. I will forever be indebted to Maureen and the Archangel Michael. I believe in the crucial importance of publicly thanking God by writing this testimonial. I hope that my story can be someone else's conversion. My prayer is that this book brings meaning and encouragement to each person who reads it and infuses every heart with the love and wonder of God!

In His Love and infinite Mercy,
Mary Ann

CHAPTER 1

Early On

God had a mission for me, and Satan knew the plan.

I was the fifth daughter of six children. My father was from Montreal and my mother was born and raised in Massachusetts. We grew up on a 100-acre farm west of Boston. My father did his best to support us as a self-employed building contractor, always struggling to find enough work to feed all of us and keep a roof over our heads.

As a small child, I remember sitting in the laundry basket on ironing day, helping my mother by handing her one threadbare garment after the other. As the youngest of five girls, every outfit had been worn by each one of us. By the time they got to me, they were worn out and out of fashion. How I wished I could have new clothes! One day as I was helping her, I remember saying, "Mom, when I grow up, I am not going to be poor."

This ambition to get ahead formed my personality into becoming a self-starter. I was motivated. I was always one step ahead of my classmates in school and knew where each lesson was headed. I found school boring and slow paced, even in kindergarten. I would have rather read a book on my own than to sit through one painful class after another. I made friends easily and enjoyed the social aspect, but the teaching methods in school were so repetitive and monotonous to me that I soon dreaded going. I begged my parents to let me drop out. My teachers never addressed my frustration, I was never told I was smart, nor did they encourage me to feel a sense of achievement. I was not tested, to see if I could skip a grade, and each year became more tedious for me. My constant complaining finally convinced my parents to let me drop out of school and join the work force instead. Now I knew I would shine.

In addition to working a series of jobs, I started to help my father remodel houses alongside my brother, and I loved it. A creative side in me was awakening. I peppered my poor father with questions about the building process, and he took the time to answer every single one of them. I enjoyed creating a new layout and seeing the completed result. I loved turning something old and worn out into something new and beautiful. My dad taught me all he knew about the building profession and I developed a great love for building things. Although I was not in school, I was still learning, and absorbing everything I could about this exciting trade, and I was thriving for the first time in my life.

This satisfaction led me to become interested in other aspects of the working world. I started saving my money. For the next three years, I worked at convenience and grocery stores earning very little. In the course of this work

I witnessed people shoplifting which led to a desire to become a store detective. I expressed this desire to a police woman that I had met and she helped me get a job doing so at a large department store. Within two years, I was number one in apprehensions! I was eventually recruited by a larger company who paid me a better salary. This, in turn, led me to write a training manual; I became the training director for the state of Massachusetts. Eventually, I moved to a very large company and was working full-time as their director of loss prevention.

During this time, I was also building, remodeling and flipping houses on the side. My responsibilities left no time for partying like others my age and I was a "straight arrow," never drinking or smoking. My drive and ambition was fueled by the desire for financial security. I was becoming a workaholic and my primary focus was on working and earning money. I was on my way to making something of my life and living in the abundance I could only dream of as a child. As I look back on this part of my life, there were three events of divine intervention that stood out protecting my life for my ultimate mission. In my wildest dreams, I could never have imagined the turn my life would take.

Most of my early memories from childhood are somewhat vague. My mother later related one story from 1962 when I was three years old. I became very ill. I ran a high fever and was hospitalized. The doctor who examined me told my mother very gravely, "This child is very sick and dehydrated. She needs to be admitted. We will do our best to save her, but we can not promise you anything." The doctors did not think I would live, but miraculously I survived. After my recuperation in the hospital, my mother recalled that I had asked her if she had brought my most prized possession, my favorite red shoes, a sure sign that I would be going home.

The second time my life was spared was while I was working in loss prevention. I tried to apprehend an older man shoplifting and when I approached him, he took a gun out of his pocket. He pulled the trigger but thankfully, no bullet fired! I radioed the police and when they came to arrest him, they opened the gun and saw that the bullet had jammed, preventing its release.

Then in 1986, while working at a department store, as Director of Loss Prevention, one of my daily responsibilities was to take the deposit to the bank at noon. But on this particular morning, as I pulled into my parking space, something unusual happened. I got out of my car, and as I was walking toward the building, my car alarm went off. I quickly ran back to my car and tried to shut off the alarm, to no avail. One of my co-workers heard the alarm and helped me by disconnecting the horn wire. I then phoned the dealership and was told to bring the car to the dealer at noon. "Just go ahead and get your car fixed," my boss told me, "and I will take the deposit to the bank." "Don't forget to take someone with you," I reminded him, as was our usual protocol. When I arrived at the dealership, oddly enough, they found nothing wrong. As I drove back to work, I noticed the parking lot was filled with flashing lights, employees, and police officers. They were surrounding my boss, who was lying on the pavement bleeding, but still alive. I was shocked to learn that he had gone alone to the bank to make the deposit. I had taken the bank deposit at noon daily, for thirteen years, without incident. This day as my boss took the deposit, in my absence, he was robbed and shot. I realized that it was the third time I had escaped death. At this time, I was oblivious to God's plan for me. I would later learn that God was protecting me for the mission He had planned for my life.

CHAPTER 2

An Unwanted Entity

I loved my job as director of loss prevention and enjoyed the extra money I earned through real estate. Of course, this meant that I needed to work seven days a week, but I was becoming addicted to the lifestyle of a workaholic and all its financial rewards. I am not sure how I found the time, but I managed to meet a man and date for five years. In 1984 we were married by a Justice of the Peace. In 1991, my husband and I started construction on our million dollar dream home. We chose a top architectural firm and they created an absolutely beautiful home with a layout that was perfect for our lifestyle. We spared no expense and gave it all the custom features and amenities possible. I managed every last detail. It truly was everything we ever wanted in a home. We could not wait to move and in May of 1992 we did just that.

Thus my journey began.

At the time the house was under construction, some very unusual occurrences began happening. I went to the lot where the new house was soon to be built. I had some instructions for the excavator who was in charge of digging the hole and pouring the foundation. I was driving my blue SUV with my Dalmatian, Sparky along side of me. He was a good companion. When we arrived at my lot, I let the dog out of the car as usual. He was well behaved and always stayed right next to me. Not this day though, for as soon as I let him out of the car he laid his ears back frightened, started howling and took off as fast as he could. Thinking back, something or someone caused sheer terror in my dog. As I was walking toward the excavator, a chill went through my body. I had an ominous feeling as if something evil was present there. Believe me, at this point in my life, this was the last thing on my mind as I was "all business" but the feeling was palpable. As I was walking around the lot, I heard the screeching of a car slamming on its brakes. Sparky came running back, trembling. He had narrowly missed being hit! I concluded my business on the property, all the while feeling an oppressive heaviness. When I got into my SUV I felt it there, too.

During the construction process, I felt this same dark, heavy feeling whenever I was on the site. I continued to dismiss it as nothing, and moved forward with the construction of our house. During the building process, one of the plasterers fell from the cathedral ceiling after one of the fiberglass boards had snapped (in spite of being purposely designed not to break.) Fortunately he did not suffer any broken bones, but needed stitches on his bloodied chin. Shortly afterwards, the carpenter who did all of our finish work partially amputated his finger on a ban saw in a gruesome accident. When he was released from the hospital he told me, "Maureen, it was almost like 'something' pulled my finger into the blade!" I just chalked it up to bad luck and busied myself with shopping for furniture, window treatments, and the furnishing of our new home. In what seemed to be the start of a wonderful next chapter of our lives, it would soon turn to true terror. I had no idea what was about to unfold. In the next few years, I would encounter the supernatural in a way I never thought possible. I would be tormented to the brink of my sanity and this malevolence would destroy my health. But I was also going to be swept up and rescued by God Himself and given an incredible gift and mission. As good things sometimes come in disguise, first, I would suffer.

On the first night in our new home, my cordless phone, still in the box and unconnected, started ringing at 1:00 AM. Half asleep, and out of habit, I reached down to the opened box beside my bed and answered it. A man's voice spoke, but I could not understand the language. It gave me an uneasy feeling, but I hung up and fell back to sleep. When I got up the next morning and stumbled on the phone box, the hair stood up on the back of my neck. I thought, did that really happen? The phone was not even connected! It felt so real and the memory was so clear. I shrugged it off as exhaustion from the day before and got back to work. I connected the phone and tried to shake off this uneasy feeling. Maybe my crazy work schedule was finally catching up to me and I needed some time off.

The telephone rang the next night. This same man with the strange voice and unidentifiable language tried to talk to me. During the day, as I was speaking to siblings or friends on the telephone, he would often interrupt and try to talk as well. Of course, only I could hear him. This was all designed to endlessly frustrate me. "Did you hear the phone ring last night?" I asked my husband. He had not. I told him about the calls but he assumed it was a wrong number. That made sense to me until one day, the voice left a gruff, unintelligible message on the answering machine. I thought, now you are captured! My husband would believe me now! I played the message five times, just to make sure it was on the recorder. When my husband got home, I met him at the door with the proof. "I want you to hear this," I told him, handing him the answering machine. "Play it!" I said confidently. He pressed the 'play button' but there was no message of any kind on the recorder. We just looked at each other bewildered.

As the days progressed, a figure of a man would come to me at night, saying nothing, just showing himself with an eerie glow. This would happen several times a week. I was beyond terrified. One night my bed shook violently. I awoke to see this dark figure with the ominous glow staring down at me. I was frozen with fear. Time and time again, I kept pleading with him, "Please, go away! You're scaring me!" I would cry. Then he would slowly fade away. He usually came as a shapeless dark form, but sometimes appeared as a man. On one occasion, I woke up to see him dressed like a Royal Canadian Mountie with a campaign hat, high boots and riding jodhpurs. I could not see his face. My bed would shake and I would plead with him saying, "Go away, why are you doing this? Who are you?" The ugly shape with the eerie glow would continue to stare down at me and eventually fade away. This entity would not only manifest himself to me almost every night, but other strange things began happening too. I would leave my house for work and when I returned, things had moved from one location to another. The lights would flicker, turn on and off and the toilet would flush by itself. Normally, I would take my shoes off at the door when I got home, and sometimes later, I would find the same pair of shoes in the middle of my backyard. On my way home, I would stop to get my mail from the side of the road and place it on the front seat of my car. By the time I drove up the driveway and opened the garage door, the mail had been moved from the seat of my car to the middle of my garage floor. Despite my anxiety and wakeful nights, my husband never felt the shaking of the bed and remained oblivious to all these frightening incidences. I started begging him to move out of the house but he insisted I was imagining things.

I raised two beautiful tiger and white cats that had been litter mates. They were strictly indoor cats. I found them to be wonderful pets and they brought me much comfort during these disturbing times. I found many occurrences when my poor cats were targeted as well. Whenever I would go shopping, my cats would always be sitting on the top of the stairs waiting for me to return home with a warm welcome. One cold winter day I returned home and my cats were nowhere to be found. Immediately I suspected something was wrong and frantically started searching for them. I looked everywhere in the house and found nothing. I then heard a faint cry and followed the direction until I found them both locked out on my screened in porch in freezing temperatures! Another time when I found them missing it took me one day and one night before I found them! Again it was in the dead of winter and they had been put in my garage. When I found them they were huddled together in the corner under some paper shivering. Needless to say they were so happy to see me and get back into the house by the warm pellet stove. On another occasion I had not been sleeping so well so I decided to leave them in the living room for the night so they wouldn't disturb me. I closed my bedroom door and was trying to doze off when suddenly I saw one of my cats in mid air over my bed; then she was just dropped on top of me! Several other times I would be on the couch watching television with the cats curled up next to me when one of them would be picked up by an invisible force and hurled across the room!

Understandably, it would be difficult for anyone to believe what I was experiencing. Without my husband witnessing any of this, I felt alone and devastated. I lived in absolute fear and I knew for certain that these happenings were real. Odd things continued to intensify in nature, but not on any kind of schedule. There was no way to predict whether a day would be normal or bizarre. I would have two or three weeks of relative peace, then the activity would resume. My wet towels would be taken from the hamper and put on the carpet, by my side of the bed. I would put them back in the hamper, leave the room and once again, find them on the floor in the same place by my bed. Being meticulous, I knew I would never have been so careless. Objects would recklessly fly around the room. I kept a key above the bathroom door and several times the key would be thrown on the floor in the middle of the bedroom. One night I heard a gurgling sound coming from the bathroom. I carefully crept to the bathroom and switched on the light. Instantaneously, water shot out of the toilet and hit the ceiling with the force of a fire hydrant! My heart leapt to my throat. It took me a minute or two to catch my breath. I knelt down and mopped up the water with some towels as quietly as I could, fearful of waking my husband. One day while vacuuming, I saw a spoon fly off the counter and across the room. Now I was becoming more alarmed, fearful of what might happen next. I could always feel this entity's menacing presence and when I sensed it near me, I would tell it to leave, but it would not. I was afraid to stay in my house alone and gave up trying to share with my husband what I was enduring.

On one particular night, I was relieved to see that my husband had arrived home ahead of me. It was such a relief to know I would not be alone in the house. As I gathered my things from the back seat of my car, I could hear instrumental music coming from the house. When I entered, the sound was in every room although our stereo was not wired to travel that far. It was not like any music I had ever heard before; I couldn't even identify the instruments. I was trying to figure out where this strange music was coming from and how to make it stop. I thought if my husband witnessed this he might believe there truly was some type of disturbance in the house. I could hear the water running in the shower. As soon as I put my hand on the bathroom door knob the music instantly stopped.

I opened the door, and my husband wondered why I had such a confused look on my face. Feeling defeated I just said, "What would you like for dinner?" I was so frustrated but it was of no use trying to explain it, knowing it would just make me look foolish again. My husband was oblivious. I suffered like this with the days becoming years, as I grew more anxious and fearful. I searched libraries but nothing could explain why and what was happening. Nor could I find advice as to what I should do. After six years of what I now know were demonic attacks, I was desperate. I was slowly unraveling and my health was deteriorating.

In the back of my mind, I nurtured a fading hope that somehow, everything would just go away. But the attacks escalated. It got so terrifying that after my husband left for work at 4:00 AM each morning, I would quickly throw my clothes on and leave the house, and spend the next two hours in a coffee shop until it was time to go to work. Since this phenomenon began presenting itself in my house, I was tremendously more fearful each day and it became harder and harder for me to go home. I never knew what to expect or who I would encounter. Little did I know, it would take another year until relief was in sight.

CHAPTER 3

The Attacks Continue

I finally confided in my mother. "I can feel its power, Mom, and it is making me sick. What can I do?" My mother was shocked at my physical deterioration. Although we spoke often on the phone, she had not seen me in a while. By the time of this visit, I was forty pounds underweight. The sight of me made her lose her breath and she knew she needed to take charge. She asked if I still had the rosary beads she had given to me from a friend of our family. I said yes, but I would have to look for them. "I have never prayed the rosary. I have no idea which prayers go with which beads!" "Well, maybe you should learn," my mother said. Taking her own rosary, she explained which prayers I was to say with each of the beads. "Pray whenever you see anything unusual, it is the only thing I can suggest. That should drive it out."

Although we had grown up going to church, I somehow fell away from the habit of attending, because during my teenage years I was too busy working and trying to get ahead in the material world. I had not attended many religion classes so I knew nothing of the things of God, but I clung to this ray of hope, desperate to try anything. I went home and frantically searched through boxes, looking for the rosary beads. Once I found them they made me feel more secure and at peace. This was something tangible that I could hold in my hand that would bring me comfort, because I felt protected. I carried them around with me at all times and kept them under my pillow at night. I began begging God for help while praying on the beads as often as I could.

Right around this time my sister was going through a divorce and came to live with me for a while. As sad as I was that her marriage was ending, I was so relieved to have her close by and to have a hand to hold. Paulette is one of the kindest people I know, and although in the beginning she did not understand my plight, she was empathetic and a good shoulder to cry on. More importantly, she believed me about all of the events that had been going on. I was thankful to have her company so that I did not feel so alone. Shortly after moving in and taking a bedroom upstairs, this entity started presenting itself to her. One evening while reading in bed, Paulette saw movement out of the corner of her eye. She looked up and saw the shadow of a large dark snake, slithering across the wall. Deathly afraid of snakes, she was instantly paralyzed with fear. It slithered around the walls as she stared in horror, and then it slowly disappeared. Also just like I had experienced, when she was on the telephone, a voice would join in her conversation and speak to her in the same unidentifiable language. Of course, when she questioned the other party she was speaking with if they also heard this voice, the answer would always be "No." It would turn her bedroom lights on and off, as well as the television. This campaign of fear was now being waged against my sister.

One night, she was awoken by the feeling of something hitting her legs. She opened her eyes and the room was very dark, except for a glowing alarm clock on the dresser, reading 4:10 AM. As she looked at the time, suddenly the television began to flash on and off numerous times. She was terrified and jumped out of bed and ran down the hall to my room crying. We went into the kitchen and I tried to calm her down. After listening to her story she relaxed a bit and we then decided to go back to her bedroom. When we got to the room, the lights were turned on, which was odd since Paulette had not turned the lights on when she ran out. Armed with the rosary beads, we could immediately feel the oppressive presence of this 'thing' in her bedroom. As I placed the rosary beads on the night table, I heard a distinctive loud growl. The entity growled at the rosary beads! We gingerly sat on the bed as she described the frightening things that she had just experienced. She told me the incident began at 4:10 AM. The clock now read 5:30 AM. Yet we glanced at another clock, a battery operated pendulum one on the bureau, and the hands were frozen at 4:10 AM. The pendulum was still swinging, indicating the clock was still in motion. I called for my husband to see this, as he was still questioning these happenings. As I called for him, the hands of the clock rapidly swung around until the clock read 5:30 AM! Paulette and I looked at each other in shock and we both now realized that this entity did not want to reveal its presence to my husband.

The entity persisted in tormenting us. My husband continued to distance himself from me, as he was not witnessing any of these events nor experiencing any of the attacks. He became angry and withdrawn, which made me feel even more alone and unsupported.

The following night Paulette went to her bedroom, still fearful from the previous night's events. She got into bed and prayed to God for protection. In her own words, "A very foreboding feeling came over me. I felt something very bad was going to happen that night. I jumped out of bed, packed a bag and was about to leave for my mother's house." She tried to leave quietly, but being a light sleeper, I heard her come downstairs. "Paulette," I said, "where are you going at this hour?" She explained how afraid she was and could not bear staying another night in that bedroom. Although I understood, I was sad to see her go that night, as she was the only one I could lean on. I went back to bed and a little while later, I was awakened by my husband in the middle of the night. He said he was cold and got up to adjust the thermostat, which was on the wall across from the bed in our bedroom. When I looked at him, his body was just standing there frozen in front of the thermostat. I sat bolt upright in bed, "Are you OK?!!" I said loudly. I continued calling out his name, each time more loudly and desperate but he continued to stand there frozen. He did not respond; he just seemed glued to that spot. Suddenly, I saw a vision of him in front of the bedroom door on the opposite side of the room. His body, that was frozen moments before in front of the thermostat, now faded and became one with the vision I saw of him by the bedroom door. He finally said, "What Maureen?" "Didn't you hear me screaming for you?" I said. "No," he replied, "I did not hear anything. I was in the kitchen getting water." I was very shaken by this.

The next morning I went to work and finally shared this story with one of my coworkers. She said, "I know a woman, Maureen. She is a psychic and has done work for the police." Thinking she was very credible, I called her. She immediately described my house and my furniture; right down to the color of my drapes. She then went on to tell me that the property I had developed at one time was a farm owned by a man named Henry. She went on to tell me that Henry had buried his son, Bob, on the property. Henry was supposedly upset that I cut down his trees while developing the property. The psychic advised me, "When you go home tonight, apologize to "Henry" and ask him to leave you alone." I left work early and rushed home to talk with "Henry" before my husband got home. I went into the kitchen and called him forth. "Henry are you here?" I then heard a knocking on the kitchen ceiling. "If that is you, Henry, knock again." There was another knock. I said, "Henry please leave us alone, please stop. I'm sorry! I didn't know your son was buried on the property. My husband and I have worked very hard and I cannot tear this house down that we built. I just want peace." Suddenly, the entire house reeked of rotting cow manure. I desperately looked to see what time it was, because my husband was due within the hour. I grabbed the air freshener and sprayed the house and opened all the windows to air out the stench. It was a hot and humid

July day and the foul odor just hung in the air for several hours. Suddenly a cold wind forcefully blew through my house and a chill went up my spine. I did not understand how this could be happening or what was in my house, but I had the feeling that this communication had just made it worse. I understood later that the disturbance was Satan, not the so called ghost of 'Henry'. I had been deceived and misled by a 'psychic' who claimed to have spiritual powers.

By the end of 1997, Paulette, decided to move out permanently. She was convinced that this eerie activity would only escalate and felt forced to leave. When she returned to collect her belongings I joined her upstairs to move her things to the car. As I attempted to lift her suitcase it seemed to be cemented to the floor. We both tried to lift it together and it would not budge, no matter what we did. I ran downstairs, got the rosary beads and went back upstairs. I began to pray. Suddenly the suitcase was released from the floor. We were both shocked and surprised! Even though Paulette felt compelled to leave, she continued to support me. I was so grateful to have someone who knew that these happenings were real. These frightening attacks accelerated even more after she left. My sister understood my bizarre situation, and we knew we had to do something but we did not know where to turn. At this time, Paulette and I had no way of discerning what was taking place or how to alleviate the problem. We had never experienced anything of this nature. We did not know who to call or who could help, so when we heard of a man named Jackson, who had a 'psychic gift,' we immediately set out to find him. Jackson charged us $35 per half hour for his services. We were frequent visitors, sometimes being there for 4 hours in one session, explaining all the activity happening in my home. He would sometimes tell us to light a white candle, or a red candle, or buy a crystal, or sage the house. He felt this was a ghost, and by doing these things it would cast it out. With no one suggesting anything better, we could only go along with this plan. We would return the following week, only to describe the same problems continuing. Nothing he advised us to do had any effect at all on these attacks.

Finally after being misled repeatedly, I had an unexpected moment of complete clarity and knowledge, and I knew that I needed to visit a Roman Catholic priest. Several days later, my sister called the local Catholic church and asked if there was a priest that could bless the house for us. We were told that the priest that usually performed those tasks was away. We then started calling many churches in the area and asked if there was anyone who could help with this matter. A church of another denomination sent a prayer group over to pray with us and to rid the house of the entity. They came equipped with deliverance prayers that we were to all pray together as we walked through the house. We started praying in the garage, moved into the kitchen and then the dining room. As we were praying, 'something' forcibly started pulling my hair! The group gathered around and started praying over me. Finally this entity released my hair. We then continued on through the living room and went upstairs to the back bedroom, where some of us felt a heavy, dark, malevolent presence. We all started praying and someone from the prayer group opened the window. Precisely at this moment, some who were present, felt this entity flee out the window. For the first time, I felt a glimmer of hope and thought my life was about to change for the better. After praying throughout the house, we all felt at ease. We were confident we had been successful in ridding the house of this demonic presence. After talking a bit, and thanking them, the prayer group left. This was the first time in months that I started to feel more positive and at ease. Breathing a sigh of relief, I closed the door behind them, but I instantly froze. There, on the back of the door was a pair of evil, red glowing eyes staring back at me! My heart started pounding, I became sick to my stomach, and my legs felt weak. These red eyes stayed on the door while I clutched my rosary beads for dear life. I turned and ran out of the room as quickly as I could. I now knew this entity was not about to leave easily. I felt hopeless in the sheer terror of this unexpected moment.

I was convinced that all the problems stemmed from this house. I begged my husband to sell it, put all the problems behind us and start fresh. Initially he dug his heels in and refused to go but after much stress and arguing, he reluctantly agreed. We moved in temporarily with my mother-in-law. Our 'dream home' went on the market for less than market value because I just wanted to rid myself of it as quickly as possible. While I was in the process of moving, I was stacking boxes in my garage and I noticed my bicycle. Not thinking I had any further use for it, I decided to put it out for the trash. I organized all the refuse, including my bike and put it at the end of the driveway. The trash man came and removed all the trash including the bicycle. Several days later, I happened to look out the window and saw the bicycle was back in the road! Again, I retrieved it and put it out once again with the trash on the following Friday. This time, I waited and watched. The trash man threw the bicycle in the back of the truck and drove off. Several days later, the bicycle was back in the middle of the road! Now this would be my third attempt to get rid of the bicycle. The following week, I put the bicycle out once again. The trash man came and removed it. Thankfully, this time it did not return.

While moving things to my mother- in- law's house one day, I heard a thump and got out of my car to find a dead raccoon in the middle of my driveway. Disgusted, I took a shovel, picked up the dead raccoon and walked over to the fence and threw it into a vacant field. The next day, I was backing out of my garage and again I heard a thump. I got out of my car and saw the same dead raccoon that I had disposed of the day before. This time, I took the raccoon to the field and buried it. The following day, I found the same raccoon in my driveway again! I went to the field and looked where I had buried it. The hole looked undisturbed, but after digging a bit I discovered it was empty! I got a box, put the raccoon in it and drove several miles down the road and threw it into the woods. By this time, the raccoon was dried up and half decomposed. Again, this was my third and last attempt; the raccoon did not return this time. I was fed up, and knew it was yet another attempt by this entity to agitate and intimidate me. I was so glad to be leaving this house! We purchased another house, but it would be a few months before we could move in. I felt confident that everything would go back to normal once we were out of that house.

CHAPTER 4

The Nice Lady

In the meantime, I was carrying my Rosary beads with me constantly. They seemed to be the only source of comfort I had. One day as I prayed, the rosary began vibrating and heating up! I heard a woman's soft comforting voice, speaking into my right ear. The nice lady repeated several times: "You have been chosen; you will help people who are in need." She had the most gentle voice I had ever heard. She reassured me that the entity in my house would flee, when I no longer had any fear of him. "How can I help people, when I am so sick?," I asked her. "I can not eat, I've lost weight and I am afraid of what might happen next!" She reassured me that all my health issues would be lifted by her Son shortly after I was settled into the new house. I prayed to her every day. She would reassure me that everything was going to be okay, and once I moved, her Son would come to me. Her Son? At this time, I had no idea who I was speaking to and no idea who her Son was. I suggested to my sister that we continue to look for a priest that could explain what was going on.

Paulette suggested that the next time the "nice lady" came to me, that I should ask her which priest we should go to.

The next day, I started praying on my rosary beads and once again they began to vibrate. The "nice lady" started speaking to me in a soft voice and repeating the same message as before. "I need a priest, where can I go?" I asked. "Go to the Shrine. There will be a priest that will know exactly what it is you are speaking of." At this point, I was suffering with anxiety and lower back pain. I felt too sick to leave the house, so my sister decided to go to the Shrine without me. Not wanting to ring the rectory door bell, she wandered into the gift shop and began speaking with the woman at the counter. "My sister is hearing voices," she blurted out, "I think she has demons in her house!" The woman did not laugh, nor turn away. "Oh, you want to see Fr. Aniello," she told Paulette, "He is a very gifted priest. He hears Jesus. Bring your sister to him." He hears Jesus??? Paulette could hardly believe her ears. Was there actually a priest who would listen to their story and understand? She made an appointment and a few days later we went back to the Shrine to meet Fr. Aniello Salicone. As sick as I was, I was determined to force myself out of bed and meet with this priest who might understand my plight.

Finally, I was face to face with Fr. Aniello. He was a wise, charismatic man, with a distinct Italian accent. Right away he put me at ease. We went into a small office and I told him everything I had been experiencing, right down to the last detail. I wanted to make sure he fully understood the magnitude of what I had been enduring for so many years. Nothing that I shared seemed to shock him or make him suspicious of me. I could tell that he believed everything that I was telling him. Every so often, his gentle nod of understanding brought me such relief to know that I was truly being listened to. After patiently listening to all that I was telling him, we both paused and there was complete silence in the room. We both closed our eyes and prayed.

I begged the nice lady who had been speaking to me, to please advise this priest that I was telling the truth and to help me. Her soft voice reassured me. Meanwhile, (as I later learned) Fr. Aniello was praying to Jesus and asking if I was mentally ill. Jesus answered, "No, my son, she has been chosen by me. I sent her to you." All the while my sister, Paulette, sat there in this surreal moment thanking God for leading us to the priest who could possibly help us. "Now I feel better!" he suddenly exclaimed, as he had just received his answer from Jesus. He then went on to ask me if I knew who the woman was that I had been speaking to. I shook my head, not having any idea. He said, "You have been speaking to the Blessed Mother, the mother of Jesus, Jesus is telling me that when you go home tonight He would like you to pray directly to Him, as He would like to talk with you." He went on to explain that demonic activity had been directed at me because Satan knew I had been chosen and that I would eventually be waging war against him. I had so many questions. I asked him why the psychic woman and Jackson, who both seemed so knowledgeable in the spiritual realm could not help me. He educated me in what he called "self-taught spirituality." He explained that there are both good and bad angels and both of them are pure spirit and highly intelligent.

Anyone can learn to make contact with them, however opening oneself up to that communication without having guidance and discernment leaves one vulnerable to the deceptions of Satan. While both of these psychics appeared to have known so much about me they were actually unknowingly communicating with Satan and Satan knew these details about me, too. This scared the daylights out of me, but Fr. Aniello's gentle demeanor assured me that everything would be alright.

This was the beginning of a lifelong friendship with a very gifted priest. Fr. Aniello told me that he had to go away for a month but he would be back in late September and we would resume our meetings then. He also told me to journal anything that was told to me by the Blessed Mother or Jesus. "This may be a book one day," he said. That night, after I went home, I started to pray. "Jesus, I was told to pray to you, to go directly to you." Not knowing what else to say, I said, "Here I am!" I sat in silence. Suddenly, I heard a very soft but strong, peaceful, loving voice. The entire room was calm and I felt a sense of peace and love going through me that was indescribable. Jesus said, "Thank you for coming to Me. You have been chosen. Learn not to be afraid. You are of the light, there is hope for everyone, these three things are most important. You will show many people hope." I explained to Him what I was going through and that my family did not believe that I was being tormented and attacked by Satan. He said, "Your family will not judge or they will be judged." He went on to tell me that all of my health problems would be lifted and He would always protect me. He said, "You will learn patience and kindness to others. It will be long hard work and you will be tired at times." He also told me, it would be my choice whether I wanted to accept this work or not. I immediately replied that I would be more than happy to do His work. I anxiously accepted this. I had no idea what Jesus' definition of long hard work was. But most of all, I did not realize at the time that much of the work I needed to accomplish, was within myself and I needed to grow in holiness.

I just could not understand why Heaven had chosen me. I was a nobody, had not practiced my Catholic faith and had little education. He told me I had been chosen for my endurance and that He and His Mother would start teaching me soon. He said, "Many people are waiting, you must learn to trust in Me." He kept repeating to me over and over, "Do not be afraid." I would soon understand.

CHAPTER 5

Have No Fear

The days progressed and the new house was nearing completion. I was so sick but I tried to stay as focused as I could on completing the renovations.

It was September and finally time to get into our newly renovated house. I started moving some of my clothes. As I carried boxes from my car to the house, I suddenly noticed the hallway closet door that had been open, was now closed. The bathroom door that I had fully opened was now also closed. I started to tremble inside. I knew there was no room for denial... I stood frozen with fear. My breathing became shorter, my legs felt weak as my entire body seemed to have an endless adrenaline rush. I dropped the box I was holding and ran to my car and drove to the nearest parking lot. I called Fr. Aniello, but there was no answer. I felt a sick twisted feeling in my stomach. I was panicking so I told myself I had to pull it together. I took a deep breath, called again and left a detailed message on his answering machine. Fr. Aniello, not knowing I had called from my cell phone, left a message at my mother-in-law's house on her answering machine. He then called me on my cell phone and explained,

"Maureen this has nothing to do with the house, this is the evil one. *You* are under attack!" This was the worst news I could hear. Why hadn't I figured this out before I sold our dream house and turned our lives upside down! He then told me he had left a message on my mother-in-law's answering machine. I felt nauseous. This caused additional stress for me, as my husband still did not believe me and his mother thought I was imagining everything. I rushed to her house and asked her if anyone had left a message for me, but she said the light on the answering machine was not flashing so there were no messages. Shortly thereafter, she left the house and I hit the replay button on the machine. Sure enough, there was the message from Fr. Aniello. Thankfully no one had heard it. He said, "Maureen, please do not to be afraid of this, we will talk." Phew! I instantly knew that there must be a good angel watching over me!

I would soon learn that Father Aniello was a very gifted priest belonging to the Xaverian order, and experienced in understanding the gifts of the Holy Spirit. As a small boy, Jesus would come to him and speak with him, and it was this unique relationship with Jesus that led him to the priesthood. God gave him the gift of healing along with other gifts and he started a ministry to help heal people spiritually and physically. He humbly said, "Love others like Jesus loves. I do not heal, God does it." Soon after, Fr. Aniello invited me to witness the works of Jesus. I began accompanying him to numerous healing services. I would witness other people being healed, but never myself. I became so frustrated and impatient but never gave up hope. I asked Fr. Aniello why I was not receiving a healing and he replied, "Perhaps our Lord Jesus was speaking of a spiritual healing and not a physical healing." I could not accept this! I said, "Fr. Aniello, I know what the Blessed Mother told me and I trust and believe I am going to have a physical healing!" "Well, then keep praying to Our Jesus and do not give up hope!" he kindly replied. I continued to attend the healing services. I would go to the shrine in all types of weather and walk through the grounds pleading for a healing. One day I told my sister, "I know I will be healed because Jesus must be so tired of listening to me!" Despite my disappointment, I remained persistent and persevered in my petition. Jesus would eventually heal me, but it was not in His plan to heal me instantly. This was the first lesson I needed to learn, never to give up hope and to continue to pray. Fr. Aniello had told me, that Jesus knows what is best for us and if we do not receive what we are asking for, He will give us something better. Jesus hears all of our prayers and will answer them in His time and according to His Will.

One night my husband suggested, "The next time this "thing" manifests itself to you, wake me up because I want to see it." At this time I continually prayed and begged God, "Please help me Jesus, rescue me, please protect me from this evil!" Several nights later, Satan manifested himself to me. I tried to sit up, but my body was frozen in place and I could not speak. I tried to scream for my husband as I heard the devil's voice speaking to me in a growling sound. "So Maureen, you want help? Ha Ha Ha!"

Satan was trying to intimidate me and make me feel hopeless and abandoned by God. I did not know what to do. My soul was calling for Jesus and the Blessed Mother, for now I knew who she was, "Please Jesus, help me, my Mother help me!" Before my eyes, white streams of light were shooting across the room, like the Fourth of July and immediately my body was freed. The entity had fled. I then heard the Blessed Mother's voice, "It is I." I thanked her profusely and then pleaded with her for help with my ill health. She reminded me that her Son promised to heal me. The next morning, I tried to explain to my husband that I could not wake him, as he had requested because my body and voice were frozen during the attack. He said, "Are you sure you weren't dreaming?" I knew I had been wide awake.

Satan was persistant, however. I was in my office a few nights later and felt the evil presence again. I felt uneasy. I looked up and there across my desk, was an unshaven man with a hooded black cloak and a crooked nose. He was sitting there staring at me. I stood my ground and I stared back at him, knowing that this was a very dark entity. I told him to "Flee, get out of here!" He stayed for several minutes and then faded away. That night after going to bed, I went into a type of dream state that was completely realistic. This dark entity threw me down the stairs and held me down in the kitchen. He pinned my head against the counter top, tighter and tighter. He was pressing on my head, like a vice. The pain was excruciating. I was frantically calling for Jesus to help release me from this choke hold. Jesus did not answer nor did He help me at that point. Finally, not being able to take the pressure on my head anymore, I kicked this entity with all my might. I was fed up, angry and I fought back with all my strength. He suddenly released me and completely disappeared. I called for Jesus, and said "Jesus where were you?" "Pity to the man who does not think My angels can not do their job." Jesus replied.

It was then that I realized that this was the beginning of my training and my next lesson was to have no more fear of this evil by confronting it head on. I now had the confidence to handle this kind of attack. At night, when all was quiet, I would pray and the Blessed Mother would come with words of encouragement, "What you are going through is normal. You must fight this, for we all have to deal with him (Satan). Fight this, build more endurance, we are behind you." She also reassured me, that I had full protection and that she and her Son would guide and watch over me. She repeatedly told me, "Have no fear of this." I have learned the more afraid we become and the more attention we give to demonic manifestations the more their activities will increase. Fr. Aniello taught me, when I witnessed any of these occurrences to say, "Thank you Jesus for loving me." Then ignore it. The Blessed Mother would encourage me to sit quietly and pray the Our Father and the Hail Mary and trust that her Son would lift this. I was to focus on Jesus not Satan.

These are just a few of the attacks that I endured within this seven year period. Satan was persistent and unrelenting. I believe Satan was trying to wear me down so

I would give up. Make no mistake about it, these attacks persist even into the present day, but I now know how to deal with them and I have no fear. Satan knew, if he could discourage me, perhaps I would abandon the mission that God had set forth for me.

CHAPTER 6

The Healing

It was mid October and New England was ablaze with color. I longed to get outside and enjoy the beautiful weather, but I had become too ill. My body was racked with pain and I did not know how much more I could take. It had been a hectic few months between moving, living with my mother-in-law, renovating a new house and organizing it. I was absolutely depleted and being so sick, it took every ounce of strength to get through it all. Even a healthy person would have been overwhelmed with the changes that I was going through. I often could not wait for the day to end so I could crawl into bed, hold onto my rosary, and rest my aching back.

It was October 14, 1998. I was not feeling well and went to bed early. I was praying when my rosary started to heat up and vibrate. Suddenly, it was like a huge stereo had been turned on and the room was filled with millions of voices, joyfully singing and repeating, "Jesus is coming, He's coming, He's coming! Jesus is coming!" I quickly sat up in bed. In an instant, to the left of my bed, was Jesus! He was kneeling and had on a red robe, sandals and had brown wavy hair. He had an olive complexion, looked to be in his early thirties and very strong. While staring at His profile I saw His hands in prayer form. "Jesus, please help me, I am so sick, please help me!" I begged. "Pray My Love, pray," He answered. He started to pray the 'Our Father' and I followed. I closed my eyes as we prayed, and I was so full of joy, knowing Jesus and I were actually praying together! At the same time because I was so sick, I was also asking Him to help me. When we finished praying, I opened my eyes and Jesus had vanished. I called to Him, "Where are you, Jesus?" Instantly I heard His voice, "You will now get back to full strength." I tried to get out of bed slowly, as I was accustomed, due to my painful back condition. Again, I heard Jesus' voice, "Get up! You no longer have pain." I stood up next to the bed. I then heard Him say, "Bend over and touch the floor." I bent over, with absolutely no pain and touched the floor! I was ecstatic! What a relief! Then I heard Him say, "I promised you a healing, now you will be able to eat."

I was so underweight and frail from barely eating; It would be a good day if I could keep down a couple small bites of food. I suddenly remembered what the Blessed Mother had said months before that her Son Jesus would lift my health issues and heal me when I was settled in my new home. The next morning, I could not wait to call Fr. Aniello and tell him of my amazing encounter with Jesus. After we spoke, he went into the chapel and prayed about this experience. He confirmed to me that this indeed was Jesus. He continued, "I then asked Jesus why He did not use me as the instrument, to heal you. Jesus told me, 'I wanted to do this Myself, son.' "I asked him why Jesus prayed the 'Our

Father' prayer. He explained that when Jesus' disciples asked Him how to pray, this was what He taught them.

That night I prayed and thanked Jesus for healing me. I heard His peaceful voice, "We must go slowly, we must stay together, we can't rush, all in time, learn our ways. It is My wish to have you pray with me every day. We pray as one, you will pray and I will pray with you and then we are as one. Our Father is whom we will pray to as one. I will lead you. You have been given prayers by Our Father." Now He was teaching me.

I was still underweight from being so sick, but now all I wanted to do was eat. All my strength and stamina came back and I was so grateful to Jesus for giving me my life back. Getting well felt like I was getting out of prison and back to enjoying life. One of my favorite things to do was to go to the Shrine and walk around the beautiful grounds. One morning, I found myself in front of the Blessed Mother's statue, and I lovingly started speaking to her in silence. I was not speaking to the statue; it was just a physical reminder of her like a picture in one's wallet. All of a sudden the sun dropped down below the statue, encircling it with dazzling rays of light that swirled towards me. The Blessed Mother said audibly in my right ear, "When you call me, I will come. This will be our agreement. Every time you call, I will come. Know that I hear all." She said again that I had been chosen and I would show others her world. I confessed to her that I felt no one would believe me. She asked me to bring my sister to the shrine, so the next day, Paulette and I returned. It was a rainy day. We ran right up to the same statue and started to pray, but I told the Blessed Mother that I had forgotten my rosary beads. She said, "Look up." Instantly, she manifested a pair of wooden rosary beads on the gate before us. She instructed us to kneel and pray the rosary. After we prayed one decade of the rosary, I heard her say, "We will show your sister now, how we shine!" Suddenly the rain stopped, the clouds parted and the sun came through, dilating and pulsating. The Blessed Mother said, "See how we shine!" She repeated this a few times. To our utter amazement, the sky turned a bubble gum pink color, then purple, then a beautiful golden color. It was just incredible and so unexpected to us both. The Blessed Mother asked me to bring my mother the following day and she would show her too. So the next day, I brought my mother. The Blessed Mother instructed us to kneel and pray our rosary. After the rosary, she said, "I will open the sky now for your mother and show her, how we shine." I was witnessing nature obey her commands. She would say that she would part the clouds, and the dark clouds parted. She announced that the sun would come out, and suddenly there was the sun! Then the sun began to dance and it started to dilate and pulsate! The sun was coming towards us quickly and then receding back into the sky! She repeated this three times. After this miracle, she turned the whole sky bubble gum pink. My mother could not believe it and was so excited she was speechless. As we looked at each other, our skin tones were emanating different colors.

The Blessed Mother then directed me to another statue of herself on the shrine grounds, where she was depicted kneeling in prayer. "In the middle of the folded hands is a gift for you." she said. I looked in the statue's hands and there was a small smooth pink translucent stone and a Miraculous Medal.* She said, "This is for you, take it. My Son knows that you will master all your training and help to show others the way."

* See the back of the book for a description of the Miraculous Medal.

CHAPTER 7

My Training Begins

November 21, 1998

I was so grateful to the Blessed Mother for all the time she took to help me. I began asking her what I could do for her. Her reply would always be, "Love, kindness, peace, joy and happiness. These would be the biggest gifts you could give me." Upon awakening the next morning, she told me, "Our Father wants you to see Him, talk with Him, pray to Him. He wants your hand. You will show others the way. You will bring them home. You will help others." She continued, "To help our people you must have compassion, love and beauty." I asked her how this would be done. She said that it would happen "through prayer." I was committed and eager to learn, but still wondered, why me? Much later, I was told by Fr. Aniello, that God works best through the lowly and can show His power and mercy better this way. I thought "Well God could not have chosen a more lowly person!"

At night, when my mind was quiet and receptive, Jesus and the Blessed Mother would come and teach me different lessons of love through dreams. When I would awaken, they would explain what the dream meant and speak of their world. Jesus spoke of how many people had strayed from His Kingdom. He said, "I will direct you but it is up to you to follow. I have some who are loyal, some who come and go and some who don't come at all. I expect loyalty to Me and companionship. Walk with Me." He explained, "Challenges we will face together, not giving up is our fight. A life of love and fulfillment is most important, then all else will follow. Fear nothing and love. Always remember My words, Life without love is not our way." Jesus explained to me that when He was on earth, Divine Love was His courage through difficult and good times. "Our journey is of peace, love and joy. Love all (for you) to be ready, perfect yourself." Other times I would be given short messages to ponder. I was told, "When all is said and done, the world will love as one." During another lesson I was told, "All is one, and one is all, with Jesus." Wanting me to totally comprehend this, I would hear this many times from both Jesus and Mary over the course of my training.

The Blessed Mother kept encouraging me to "Learn the fruit." I had no idea what she meant. She continued, "After you learn this you will be able to go out into the world and help others." "I will strive to perfect this," I eagerly replied. "You are the warmth of my heart, keep learning, I long for this," she said. Wow! The Blessed Mother longed for my love (as she longs for all her children's love.) It would be through her unfailing love that she would give me encouragement to continue on with my training. I asked Fr. Aniello, what the Blessed Mother meant when she said "Learn the fruit", he explained that the fruits were love, joy, peace, patience, kindness, goodness, faithfulness, gentleness, and self-control." Now I realized why Heaven kept repeating this and it suddenly dawned on me that this would take time as I had a lot to work on within myself.

I'd come to love Mary very much. She became my best friend, always there to love and comfort me, and I trusted her completely. I was so attached to her that I started to withdraw from people, and before I knew it, she temporarily withdrew from me! I called for her for several weeks but got no response. I persisted and finally, I heard her compassionate voice. "You must live your life on earth" she said. "My Mother, I'd rather be with you." She replied, "You must live your life on earth and socialize with others. You must be balanced." The Blessed Mother taught me that the biggest lesson I had to learn was the lesson of love, to learn how to love as they love. She said, "Your heart cannot love enough." They gave me the knowledge to understand why people act in various ways. I was taught that much of people's actions stem from their childhood. Lack of balance, abuse or neglect would cause insecurities within the individual. Jesus told me the way to understand perfect love, was to understand people and why they react in certain ways. One who hides his wounds is afraid they will be thought less of and lose love. The reason they continue to hide these wounds is because they want more love. He added, "One who acts in anger, is one who's usually lacking in love." The Blessed Mother then told me, "Part of your work will be to help people understand themselves with your angel's knowledge." Little by little I was starting to comprehend.

One time, Jesus spoke to me in a stern voice. I asked why He was speaking to me in this different manner. He said, "This is how you speak to others. You must learn kindness and gentleness with all." He reassured me that He would teach me these lessons, ever so gently. Jesus was teaching me patience. I learned that patience was best developed through trials. He told me He would give me nine times the endurance of which I had. I would set out on my daily tasks but I'd often, lose patience or speak in the wrong tone, which I was notorious for. I had been a workaholic and had no patience with people if they weren't efficient like me. One day, Jesus showed me the following vision. I saw His hand holding the handle of a bucket filled to the brim with sand from the times I had been patient and kind. On this day I had been very impatient and unkind and He dumped the bucket of sand out and said, "We must start all over, again." He went on to tell me, "Patience, and kindness, do what is in the best interest of the other person. Learn this and we will go on." Jesus knew exactly how to get my attention! Time and time again, Jesus would use this stern voice and then His soft voice as a way of reminding me how the tone of my voice affected people I interacted with. He said, "Speak and act carefully with others. Believe in Me, as I believe in you, so you can continue to walk on reaching out to help others." He continued "I made you, I know what you need. Love Me and My Mother and we will take care of the rest. Joy is My word to you. Spend more time with Me. Every moment you spend with Me, you have been given love, joy and peace."

The Blessed Mother told me during this period, "Mean people do not prosper and belligerent people perish." It was a year before I mastered patience and kindness to others. Jesus told me perfect love would be something I had to strive for and that it was the foundation of my training. I realized that to have perfect love, one must have no fear of anything. As I began to make sense of this, He said, "You have shown no fear.... for this I grant you peace." He encouraged me to continue with my training by telling me, "The work of which you receive will be of My world, you and My Mother will provide knowledge to those who need it. There are so many children waiting for you." The Blessed Mother would visit briefly and say, "To the power and to the glory." She told me there will be a time when, "Nothing will be worth anything, just people's services to one another." The Blessed Mother reassured me by saying, "For you will be taken care of. You will conquer all. You will have everything you need to conquer this mission and more. Most proud I am of you." Jesus then said to me, "For all of My glory... glory, for all of My blessings... blessings." "You won't recognize Me... I am coming back through My people. Through you I will show My world to our people." He always gave me great encouragement to continue especially when I was struggling to understand their world.

I'd meet with Fr. Aniello several times a week, to read him the lessons Heaven was teaching me. Father would patiently listen, and would then discern them. At times, Jesus would give me scriptural messages. This would show Father that they were coming from God, because he was aware that I had no knowledge of scripture. For example, one day, Jesus told me, "Those of us who are first, will be last." Fr. Aniello was quick to point this out to me from Scripture. I had been seeing the number 711 quite frequently in visions and asked Father what it meant. Again he said to just journal it as the significance of this number would most likely unfold down the road. Fr. Aniello also taught me that there is no punishment or reward when we are on earth. I asked him to elaborate on this and he explained, "Only after our death will we have our final reward or our final punishment!"

One night Paulette and I were talking about the difficult days of my training. Trying to keep things light, Paulette jokingly said, "Wouldn't it have been much easier, if your gift was to have been a popular singer, with a beautiful voice? Think of all the appreciation you would be getting, instead of all this suffering!" We could not stop laughing! Laughter was just the medicine I needed. Later that evening, I heard Jesus say, "There is a rose at the end of the road. Your Oscar will be given to you behind the curtain." He was trying to help me understand that my reward would be in Heaven, not here. I would receive merit after I died for helping others. My days were spent in conversation with Jesus and Mary, talking about the importance of love. They were with me when I ran my errands, cleaned the house and fed the cats. It seemed I was completely immersed in the ways of Heaven and the training rarely let up.

In another dream I was shown what I was doing wrong and what I was doing right. It taught me not to tell people what they wanted to hear or mislead them, but to speak the truth, to be honest and straightforward, but loving and gentle. Jesus told me never to judge another person, for only He knew the heart and the soul of that person. He said, "I will judge what a sin is." Some dreams showed me I became too agitated if things didn't go my way. I had to change this or I could not do God's work. I still had to work on patience, humility, understanding, and not take anything personally.

One night in a dream state, I saw myself on a plane and I opened the door. Before me was a rope ladder with a very angry woman clinging to it. Behind her were more people. She was screaming loudly, "Let me in!" She pushed all the other people behind her further back. Because of her anger, Jesus let her rope go further out into the air, knowing that he would bring her to safety once she calmed down. Finally, Jesus brought her inside the airplane and told her, "Those of us who are first, will be last, remember this."

Jesus showed me a vision of many trees with a lake behind them. I asked what this meant and He said, "Now you can see the water. The trees stand for obstacles. You will have obstacles you will have to overcome." Then in a dream I'd see myself telling my story and the person doubting me. Jesus said, "You will have this in the course of your lifetime. When this happens, leave it and move along. Don't let anyone take control of your emotions." The Blessed Mother said, "You will make it. People will say things. You will have to stay in control. The more power the more you can expect criticism. People will ask how you came about this gift. You are to tell them 'Through Our

Lord Jesus!'" With a whisper she continued, "Hold on to me, our hope is that you open your heart. Let others in and Heaven will be yours."

Jesus told me, "For it is I who have not forgotten your good promise, your good thoughts and your good will." A part of my training was learning to let go of the everyday world, which was a hard teaching for me. I had to go deep within and try to detach myself from earthly attachments in order to grow spiritually. Jesus would tell me, "Learn to let go, so you can enhance the beauty of the afterlife. Grow more in your love for Me. I would move the world for you. We will show others My love and kindness." He went on to say, "How long it has taken you to come forth, for you see our beautiful work will change the world."

I saw that Jesus patiently waits for all His children. I was no more special than anyone else. Whenever Jesus or the Blessed Mother came to me, everything would become very peaceful and I would feel a sensation of love go through me that was indescribable. This feeling cannot be explained in human words nor with human understanding. My breathing would almost cease and then I would hear their beautiful voices. There was no worry, no regret, only peace. The only thing that mattered at that moment was their love and my relationship with Jesus and His Mother. As my training continued, they would come to me more frequently. Finally, after much training, Jesus came to me and said, "Victory, Victory, Victory, Glory, Glory, Glory! You have bloomed now, into a flower. Up mountains and down into the valley!"

It was Christmas Eve. I heard Jesus say ever so gently, "Speak to Me." I thanked Him for all he had done for me, for healing me, and for opening up this new world of love and truth. Suddenly, I felt a force going through my body. Above Jesus' voice, in my right ear, I heard another voice, speaking quickly and clearly. This voice was telling me about everything I'd ever wanted to know. As he was speaking, Jesus was saying to me, "This is your angel St. Michael, He will guide you." Jesus then left and Saint Michael the Archangel continued speaking to me! He answered every question I ever had from the time I was a little child to the present. He talked in detail all about my personal interests, my likes and dislikes. I was completely amazed that he knew everything about me, from my infancy to the present. It was exhilarating as I was also flooded with what seemed to be unlimited knowledge! Never tiring, he gave me clear, precise information all night long. I wanted to know more and more, especially about my health. I asked him, "My angel, Jesus came and healed me. Does this mean I will never get sick again?" I wondered if I had special protection because Jesus Himself had healed me. He explained that I had to take care of myself. I had to exercise and eat properly like everyone else. Wondering if I would ever get a cold again, he said, "Yes." He also pointed out, that my back was healed, but still susceptible to problems if I wasn't careful. He told me to avoid any heavy lifting, to be aware of correct posture and get moderate exercise. I realized that Jesus had given me back my health, but I still needed to act responsibly and take care of myself.

The angel was still speaking to me the next morning! My right ear felt hot from receiving all this information. I was completely fascinated by this conversation with St. Michael and did not want it to end. Finally, around one o'clock Jesus came and said, "You know, you must live your life as well." That reminded me that it was Christmas Day and I needed to get organized for our family dinner. Jesus assured me that I would always be able to talk with the angel. I couldn't wait to call Fr. Aniello and share the experience I had with St. Michael. Fr. Aniello was very enthused with my experience, and explained that angels are God's messengers and live to serve and worship God. It was still hard to fathom that I was communicating with Heaven. It was as if I was living two lives. I would have to learn how to adapt to this. I could speak to them and be part of their world and then go to the supermarket and be in our world. Transitioning back and forth was difficult in the beginning. I'd feel total peace when communicating with Heaven, and a stark contrast when feeling the reality of everyday life. I was seeing the world in an entirely new way and was learning how valuable each soul was to Heaven. I thought about how many were so far away from God and needed to know this. I realized I had to share with people that Heaven and Hell are real places and that they need to pay attention how they care for their souls.

My communication with Our Father, Jesus, the Blessed Mother and St. Michael is through thought. I think a question or pray silently and they respond to me audibly, in my right ear. When I see visions, I see them with my right eye. Sometimes I just receive the "knowing" or "knowledge" deep in my soul. I see Jesus, but only see a bright light when communicating with the Blessed Mother or St. Michael. Sometimes, I will just see a vision of hand motions. If a person asks me a question, St. Michael will answer if it is God's will. I have been taught to repeat exactly what I have been told to the person I am helping. No more, no less.

The Blessed Mother told me, "If you were to tell people that you see and hear me and my Son Jesus, some would doubt and not believe you. So therefore we are giving you proof." I realized that the knowledge I was receiving from the angel would be the proof. The accurate information that the angel would be able to give me would help people to believe that my gift was real. However, even with this, some people still wouldn't believe. The Archangel Michael would start by building my faith and trust in him. I needed to learn to trust that the information he was giving me was real and true. If he chose not to answer a question it was for a good reason. I would like to share a few stories that involved my training and learning, so you can get a better picture of the process God used to open up His world to my human understanding.

One day at the store as I was digging my grocery list out of my purse, I heard St. Michael's voice. It was dawning on me that my life was truly altered forever. St. Michael said in his direct voice, "You see this man in front of you? He is an auto mechanic. When you leave the store, he will get into a truck, with tires in the back." Sure enough, I would finish my shopping, go out and see the auto mechanic get into his truck, filled with tires. This exercise was happening frequently now. Then in a restaurant, St. Michael said, "You see this woman who is your waitress? She has two children, a boy and a girl. She is recently divorced." I got chatting with her and sure enough, she confirmed these details.

In another incident, St. Michael reassured me that the results of my thyroid test would be negative, and indeed it came back negative. Another time, I was in a convenience store and hanging in front of me were some instant lottery tickets. Michael said, "Buy number 9. It will be a two dollar winner." I bought number 9 and in fact, it was a $2 winner. The lesson was not for material gain, but confirmation of the information he was imparting to me. He would repeat these things over and over. It was building my faith and trust, teaching me that I could trust the message to be true. The knowledge I was getting was not to make me smarter and make my life more exciting; it was being given to me so I could help others.

Satan, knowing that I did not yet know how to completely discern, took great pleasure in trying to deceive me. I was told by him that I was going to win the lottery and feed hungry children around the world. He would mimic my angel's voice telling me, "You must first master your training before I give you the winning lottery numbers. You are not doing well enough. You must strive more." So I prayed longer, worked harder, and exhausted myself. This was all meant to entice, tire and frustrate me. I continued to ask, "My angel, when will I be done with my training?" and Satan, continually reassured me, by telling me "soon,".

One snowy night, I awoke at 2:00 AM. I didn't realize it was Satan disguising his voice as my angel's voice again. He said, "Now is your time. Go buy the lottery ticket!" I jumped out of bed and went out to my car. There was close to a foot of snow on the ground and it was still coming down. I cleaned the snow off my car and drove to purchase what I thought was the winning lottery ticket. The next day Satan came to me again, using the angel's voice. He said, "Your winning numbers are going to be drawn tonight!" I was so excited that I was about to win, I said, "I have to call Fr. Aniello and tell him!" Satan then said, "Don't tell him! Let it be a surprise!" Needless to say, the numbers were drawn that night and I did not win a thing! I was so disappointed with myself, and realized I had fallen into Satan's trap. God permitted this to show me how careful I must be, in discerning all messages from Heaven. After I relayed this story to Fr. Aniello he said directly, "Maureen, you must discern the message, not the voice!"

Another night I was watching tv and looked at my watch. It was 8:00 PM. After the program ended, I did some paperwork, and when I glanced at my wristwatch again it was 11:00 PM, so I decided to go to bed. I went upstairs, turned my bedroom light on and there in the middle of my bedroom floor, was the watch I'd just been wearing! I then heard Satan laughing, in his evil, sarcastic voice. "It's *time* for you to give up!" he snarled. I found this disturbing but it made me think I must be making spiritual progress, because he was angry. I was learning Satan's common ploys to discourage me were often by causing doubt and despair.

St. Michael said we give Satan too much credit. He said, "If we focus on Jesus as much as we focus on Satan, think how much Heaven would benefit!" I have found that many don't believe in Satan, and others see him everywhere giving him too much credit and attention. People are quick to think that when something goes wrong in their life, it's because of the influence of Satan. Often it is just part of our journey or permitted by God for the purpose of learning. I've talked with people who are convinced that every problem is a result of Satan's interference. Satan loves to get credit for all that goes wrong in this world and we shouldn't acknowledge him so much. A good way to remove ourselves from Satan's influence is to concentrate on the goodness and love of God the Father. Another way is to follow the Blessed Mother's humility and put ourselves under her protection and guidance. I pray to her every night for this.

One morning in January of 1999, I woke up, hearing Jesus say to me, "March on, March on." Therefore, I knew I still had a way to go with my training. Jesus would tell me repeatedly, "I dare not give you these gifts, without the training, for it could become witchery in the wrong hands." I was very anxious and wanted to complete my training, eager to see what would come next. I wondered what kind of work I would be doing for Jesus. I'd ask Him, "Can we move along faster now?" He would respond, "Follow My Will. This means kindness and love to all, especially those in need. You must master all of our lessons. You have gone on your path and seen your road. Practice this. Then we can move onto the next step."

Jesus would tell me, a strong belief in Him was very important. I was learning that being in a hurry did not matter to God. God was not on an earthly time schedule. I likened it to my past in the construction business. God makes sure he has a good solid foundation before he raises the house. He has a plan for each person and methodically follows through with it. I didn't understand what He was doing but I realized that He did! Once I realized this and put my trust in Him and His plan I was more at peace. I began to put God first. Now I was starting to understand the Blessed Mother's instruction when she said "Learn the fruit." Patience was the 'fruit' at the top of my list!

Again, please keep in mind, as you read the words from Heaven to me, that God always speaks to a person on their level. I wasn't very educated, I wasn't a theologian. I was just an ordinary person, and I was spoken to in words and given examples that were easy for me to grasp and comprehend.

At times when I was tired, Jesus would give me a poem such as:

"Stars are bright, Heaven is light, all My angels are in sight" or He would say, "We are walking together, hand in hand, one step in front of another, always together...for our life will be forever and ever together."

Another time when I was getting tired He told me "Listen to the word of the Lord, it is I who has given you the strength, it is I who has given you love, it is I who has shown you the way. Listen, listen, listen and all shall be said! For all of our power, for all of our life, we will set things right, but we will have to fight without fright. It is I your Lord who will command and it is you who will obey. It is you who will keep our promise of all that is to come."

St. Michael was always there when things got harder for me. He would give me encouragement in poem form, such as:

"Our love is deep, our mountain is steep, and we are still a bit weak, but soon we will reach our peak."

"Jesus, our Savior is kind to all, but wants us to stand tall, for we must not fall, for when He calls, we shall say all."

St. Michael would encourage me to pray by saying:

"Bright day, sunny way, we will always pray."

He would reassure me that, "Our love will grow for all."

He said Heaven only wanted what was best for me and others, and that this would be my new life. St Michael went on to tell me, "Our love for others must grow and for all this, we know, so as we slowly go, the world will have to know."

He would give me an inspiration in poetic form. "Our love is like a flower, it rains on every hour, so don't you see the power, of that special flower?" ...

"Broken wings, battered heart, we are ready for a brand new start."...

"Skies are blue, your love is true, for we only have a few (helpers)"...

"Snowflakes on your heart will melt, in ever so longing I have felt, your tear drops on my shoulders, as they melt."

These were all words to teach me how to love, in the right way.

Slowly I was learning Heaven's way.

February 6th, 1999
The Blessed Mother came to me with these beautiful words: "My heart is centered on you and through the years, I will watch over you. You and your angel will work together and conquer all that we put forth in front of you." She told me that She and her Son would never fail me and that I would help many people. She said they were proud of the progress I'd made so far in my training. "You will make a difference." She said ever so gently that we would be together forever and that loving hearts never separate. Again, these were words to strengthen and reassure me to continue on.

Sometimes I would see Jesus' hand, holding a flower. This was just more encouragement for me to continue. Simple, sweet things would occur at times, to soothe my tired brain from all of the training. I would always wear the Miraculous Medal that Our Blessed Mother manifested for me at the Shrine. Once in a while, I would wake up to find my hand holding the Miraculous Medal and the Blessed Mother's hand wrapped around mine. This would give me great comfort.

As I was progressing and learning, I was reminded to take care of myself. St. Michael was like my personal trainer and life coach. He would guide me even on the simplest issues like food. He went shopping with me and helped me pick out the correct foods. He pointed out what kind of foods to eat, what was nutritious and what was harmful. He told me I should be exercising, and encouraged me to take walks with him, as he knew I did not like to exercise. He guided me through all of this, step by step.

Jesus saw that I had developed a strong love for His mother over the years. He would ask me, "Will you love others, as you love My Mother?" I would answer, "Yes" and He would reply to me, "Then we will continue on." Jesus, knowing my inner struggle said, "When my mother and I were on earth, we both sacrificed our lives, for others. My mother's desire is to have peace. My kingdom cannot forget my children. My children fill my heart with love. Build your wealth in me."

Jesus told me to be careful and selective with my words. He said, "For you have seen Heaven's power now." I now realized what a huge responsibility this was going to be. As we moved forward, the Blessed Mother told me I would discover my new life more and more. "We will face all challenges together, our love is a bond and we will go on," she said.

CHAPTER 8

"You will have to sacrifice self, for the sake of others"

March 25, 1999

I was starting to become accustomed to this new way of life and I grew in faith and trust in God. He let me experience more of this reality than I ever thought existed. As the trauma of Satan's attacks fell further into the past, I felt emotionally and physically stronger. I was learning to balance my daily life with divine conversations and build endurance. I thought I understood all they were teaching me and my training would be close to completion. Little did I know how far from the finish line I was, and nothing could prepare me for what I was about to encounter next.

The Blessed Mother came to me during this time and explained that we were going to take a "Heavenly trip" to broaden my knowledge. She was going to show me Purgatory! She said, "Relax my child," and wrapped her arms around me. I felt my soul leaving my body. The next thing I knew, I was in what I can only describe as a grey area. I saw a large group of people there, although I could not make out their faces. All were wearing the same light color grey robes. The landscape and mountains in the background were also grey. She wanted me to experience Purgatory and show me that it did exist. Although there was peace about these people, they seemed to lack joy. I did notice one woman I had known, Cindy, who appeared to be struggling. I had been acquainted with her on earth; she had died a year or so before this experience. The Blessed Mother explained to me that this was Purgatory, and these people needed prayer and she visited them frequently. She had only shown me what I could digest easily at this time. After this experience I could see myself in bed with my soul going back into my body before I woke up.

Many times the Blessed Mother would ask St. Michael to give me a more detailed explanation. He told me that our deceased loved ones can pray and do more for us on the other side than they can here. Then I asked my angel about Cindy. He said, "She is in Purgatory, working on uneven love." I asked him to explain 'uneven love'. He said she had been forgiven by Our Father who is all merciful but in order to make it to Heaven one must have full love. We must love the same way God loves. Although she was sorry for harming others and had forgiven others for hurting her, she couldn't forgive herself. In order to have 'even love' one must not only forgive others but oneself as well. This was a real eye opener for me, as I realized that if we are aware of this we can make every effort to correct it before we die and shorten our stay in Purgatory.

I understood that this was a place of purification before going to Heaven. In Purgatory, people work through the sins they committed on earth; for example, how they hurt those around them. They ponder their life on earth, show sincere sorrow for their failures, and advance closer to Heaven. I realized that this is a great mercy that God gives, because of the many people who die each year with a grudge or holding on to some type of anger. I didn't realize at that point that there were other levels of Purgatory I'd be shown later.

The following evening, I had another experience of leaving my body. I could get from one location to the next in seconds. I went from my house to my mother's house (15 miles away at the time) in a moment. I saw my parents sitting on the sofa in their pajamas. Immediately, I was home going back into my body and waking up. The following day, I called my mother. I explained my experience and asked if the night before she'd been wearing her polka dot pajamas and her housecoat, and if her dog was with her on the sofa. She confirmed it all. After these two experiences, I was told by Jesus and Mary, that life always goes on. When our body dies, our soul continues on.

Mary said, "Let me tell you of our journey. Our people are in need of love and hope. Through our work we will help many people of all kinds." She told me that my life had changed and through these changes there would be glory for many. Somehow, the small sacrifices I was making to grow in virtue was making a difference and benefiting the lives of others. She taught me about our intentions. If someone was doing something not quite right but they had good intentions, they would still gain merit for it. I asked her to explain this and she said Heaven always looks at one's intentions. Was it of love, caring and kindness? Was it to help another or was it for self benefit? Was it to cheat or to steal? If someone gave someone money but the goal was to control or manipulate the other person, he or she would not gain merit for it. If one gives money in order to brag and bring attention to oneself, there is no merit in that either.

The weeks turned into months and then into years. I was not sure how much progress I'd made in Heaven's eyes and how much longer this training would take. Jesus told me that people are trying, striving, bearing a load and I had to help them by bearing my load. He said I was chosen because I could bear the load. He also said, "You've been through many trials. These trials that you have been through have been for a great purpose. All of our prayers and hope is for all. For Me to come to you and for you to accept and endure this training to help my people, you are My miracle!" He was telling me that because of these experiences I could empathize with and help others. He explained that the training would be very difficult at times, but I would feel great fulfillment in doing His will as it was for the greater benefit of all His children. He reassured me that He would walk beside me and always be with me. Satan, knowing I was getting frustrated, would try to tempt me back to an everyday life by saying, "I can give you anything...wealth, lottery numbers, real estate. Come with me. Forget about all this nonsense you are being taught. You can live on a beautiful ocean and have anything you wish." He kept reassuring me he could give me all the wealth that I desired. I responded firmly, "Flee, get out of here, in Jesus' name. I would rather be broke and sleeping on a park bench, then talking with you." I then heard Jesus loud and clear, "I have the power!" There was no way that I could ever be tempted or persuaded by Satan.

My struggle was not so much with Satan's interference, but with the length of my training. I started expressing my concerns to the Blessed Mother and Jesus, saying, "It's taking so long. I don't think I can to do this anymore." Mary reassured me that I had free will and that it was my choice, and if I decided to stop, they would still love and cherish me. Then for two to three weeks, I had no communication with them at all. I instantly felt a great void in my life and kept calling for them, asking for them, waiting for them, nothing. No visits, no messages. I started praying to the Blessed Mother and Jesus and asking them to please come back. I kept apologizing and telling them that I could not bear living without them now. The Blessed Mother was the first to respond. She said, "Are you sure my child?" I told her I couldn't imagine life not being in her presence and communicating with her. Their absence had been so difficult for me. She reassured me that if I decided not to do their work, she would always be beside me and in my heart. I wanted to resume my training and firmly told her so. She responded, "You will have to sacrifice self, for the sake of others. Your life is for all."

When I awoke in the morning I was shown the following vision. I saw Jesus standing on a hill in all His radiant splendor. He was holding a bow with one arrow, and there were many targets before Him. He turned His head and gave me a look of reassurance. He then placed the arrow in the bow, and drew back the string. With a mighty force the arrow hit the exact center of the bull's eye of every target, one right after the other in quick succession! If I had blinked my eye I would have missed it; that is how fast the arrow pierced all the targets! I was still in awe of this miraculous feat, when I heard St. Michael speaking, He said, "Be patient. When Jesus is ready to move He only needs one arrow!"

That was all it took to get me back on track. Once again, I was shown that God's timing is most definitely not our timing. I needed to remain peaceful and patient in this time of learning. God has the perfect purpose and plan for all our lives. Just like Jesus shooting the arrow, He knows the perfect time to take action. I realized I was looking for instant changes in myself, instead of trusting in God's timing. It is through this period of waiting, I was learning, that God often forms and develops us. I understood that this was something I had to achieve and it was a critical piece of my training! At times, when I wanted to give up, Jesus would come with these words, "I've always been forever. I need your voice. Many do not believe." I then got a second wind and we began our training again. Jesus said, "We are one, I am with you every moment of every day." He showed me again, when we prayed the Our Father together, we were united as one, and that it was His wish that we pray every day. St. Michael would say on occasion, when I wanted to give up, "My Little Star, what would happen if you were to die tomorrow? Take a look at yourself and ask 'Have I let go of earth's boundaries, have I forgiven, have I done the best that I can do to love God?' How much have you achieved for our world and how much merit have you achieved for yourself?" This stopped me in my tracks and I realized that I had much more work to improve myself, if I wanted to continue to do God's work here on earth helping others.

Before Mass, I would often feel the presence of the Blessed Mother beside me and I would ask her why she was there. "I have come to give you blessings," she would say, to encourage me to attend Mass and to pray. She and Jesus used every possible tool to teach me love. They would come to me and 'play' a variety of songs, knowing the music I loved. The lyrics were a teaching in themselves, with the lyrics chosen so I could understand and feel the emotion. I would be instantly inspired, energized and motivated. This meant so much to me, as it would unite me with them and their Heavenly powers. Even now, if I hear one of 'their' songs, it will instantly take me back to those memories. Jesus told me, "It is not how quickly we grow, but the depth in which we grow. We have gone quite a distance, but we still have a road ahead of us, in which we shall walk together. I have promised you my world and this you will receive."

St. Michael taught me how to pray saying, "I come to you Lord with love, I come to you Lord with faith, I come to you Lord, I come to you." Jesus would say, "I row and when I row, you must accept to ride." He was teaching me ever so gently that if I trusted Him and surrendered to His will, that He would lead and guide me. I would ask, "Am I ready yet?" He would reply, "Your love must grow stronger and stronger, for if our love is not strong and in a total bond (with us), it will not work."One day I asked Jesus, "In your world, what is the highest form of prayer?" "When you love, that is the highest form of prayer," was His reply.

Jesus and Mary wanted me to learn freedom from earth's ways, always emphasizing love and forgiveness. One day in prayer I was shown a vision of myself crying after being bullied in school. I heard Jesus' voice, "Forgive them." Once I did this, the feeling of being unjustly treated no longer had a hold over me.

From the onset of my training, I would have trouble discerning what was from Heaven and when I was being tricked by Satan. Jesus simplified this for me. He drew two parallel lines. He asked, "What did I do when I was on earth?" I answered Him, "You were a teacher. You helped the poor, healed the sick, and cast out demons, Jesus." He replied, "Exactly! So the easiest way to discern is if anything goes outside these two parallel lines, question it. Then you will know if it is coming from Me or not." St. Michael said, "The fruit that Jesus' instrument will bear, will run parallel with what He did when He was on earth." This helped greatly in discerning the messages I was receiving. St. Michael told me when I started to do their work, I had to be free from distractions and have a clear mind. This meant that I had to block out everything going on around me or in my mind at the time. I couldn't let anything disturb my peace as it would interfere with my clarity. It was only then that I could really absorb the messages. It took a lot of mental strength to stay focused when I was worried about a problem in my daily life.

One day during this same time, Jesus came to me and said, "Elijah, learn of him, he is a friend of mine." I had no idea who Elijah was. Fr. Aniello told me he was a great prophet and directed me to the Bible to read about him. After I studied Elijah, Jesus came to me and said, "Are you ready for My friend to speak to you?" I was about to learn firsthand, how Heaven speaks to us as individuals, knowing we are each unique and respond to different learning methods. God knows the best approach to get His point across to each one of us. God understood that I was a simple and straightforward person. Heaven understood that this is how I would learn best. The next thing I knew, I heard a powerful voice, saying, "I am Elijah. I have come forth with great hope and desire to do our Father's work." He continued, "Do you know how stupid you are? I said, "No, how stupid am I?" (He knew this is the casual way I would speak) "You are so stupid, you cannot even see two feet in front of you and we can see the world. He was pointing out my short sightedness in not seeing how I was to fit into God's plan. He reassured me that Jesus would guide me on the perfect path, in the perfect way and that all of this would be best for me and others. Elijah was guiding me back in the direction to help Heaven and away from my earthly desires. He finished by saying, "As time goes on you will discover your abilities more and more."

Heaven spoke to me in a way I could understand and used Elijah, who was direct and to the point, just like me.

I often went to the Shrine to walk through the beautiful grounds. It was there I heard Jesus say, "I can see the world; you cannot. I can see ahead of you; you cannot. You will work full time for our kingdom when you are ready. Put all your trust in Me. You will do My duties." The Blessed Mother said, "Blessed are the fruits. You have been loved by the Lord and chosen to show the people Our Kingdom. We have great hope that all will come forth. Our Father has bestowed blessings on you. We appreciate your hard work. Continue on, proud we are of you."

Jesus, the Blessed Mother and St.Michael continually gave me encouragement to stay the course. One Easter morning, as I awoke, St.Michael showed me a bushy tail and big ears, trying to make me laugh and cheer me up. He knew how weary I was from the last few years of my training. That morning, I did not want to get out of bed and get dressed, but St.Michael had other plans for me. I said, "St. Michael, I really don't feel like getting ready and going to my parents." He said, "No, My Little Star, up, up, up and forward!" I got out of bed, laughing and got ready for the day. Michael always knew exactly how to motivate me.

Jesus came to me with this beautiful poem, "A dove, a flower, a ton of hope, all of these are of beauty. Needless to say, beauty is very seldom seen, in any (of these things.)" Jesus said, "It will be us who will show them. Your life will be challenging. People will challenge you. Do not let

anybody bother you, in any way. People are not understanding and caring sometimes, but we must persevere
through all. Listen, listen to My words and you will not be
disappointed. Go on walking, saying that you have seen
the Lord Jesus Christ and that forever you will live in
Him! Never release anger. Always control yourself. Reveal
anger and you lose control. Rest, knowing that I am with
you. Rest, knowing that I love you." I asked, "What will
my life be?" Jesus said, "I say to you, greatness! Amen,
Amen, I say to you. Love, love, love, for that is all I am.
Never forget that I am with you. There will be many happenings, but most important is that you remain with Me."

The Blessed Mother explained this shortly thereafter,
"You will bring us glory." I then asked her again, "When
my training is completed, what will I be doing for you?"
She replied, "I will reveal this when you are ready to accept it."

CHAPTER 9

"Your real treasures are in my world"

I'd always been frugal and saved my money, and that allowed me to survive financially while I was undergoing my training with Heaven. One day, I asked St.Michael to tell me which stocks to buy. "What makes you think you are any different than the man across the street?" was his quick reply. He explained to me that I had a spiritual gift from Heaven and not to expect any material gain from it. Knowing that my next question most likely involved real estate, he continued, "You have to be willing to do our work. We will not send you real estate. You will live your life like everyone else! You have a desire to want real estate, your soul does not. You must have a purpose when you make money. When we work... it is for Jesus."

Another time I boldly asked, "Jesus can you send me the winning lottery numbers, or can you send me a piece of real estate?" His response was, "The rich will not even nod to the poor. I would walk through fire for you. Wealth does not bring happiness. I will show you our world." He followed up by saying, "Make the best out of what I send to you no matter how small or big, always do what My Heart would do. Better things lay ahead for you, I will send you our world, look beyond the material." I was learning that I would serve God by serving others not by serving myself. He was more interested in my being strong spiritually on the inside and focused on Him. This would enable me to cope better with what was happening on the outside. He was teaching me that our close relationship with God was the most important. I was slowly but surely beginning to understand material wealth was of no consequence in His world.

In God's eyes, all people are equal. Because I was being trained to be an instrument for Heaven did not make me any more worthy or special than anyone else. St. Michael said if he helped me buy and sell real estate, it would only serve my purpose and not God's purpose. He then continued, "When Jesus was on earth, His life was for all and His Father would only send the material when there was a need." He was trying to make me see that it was fruitless to pursue superficial meaningless things, selfish goals, and frivolous interests. I asked St. Michael how I was doing now with my training. He said, "Your short temper has prolonged us, but you have grown so far. It is time for us to help you. Look before you; what is it that you are wanting? Is it our world or the material world?" "It is your world, my angel," I confidently told him. "Okay, My Little Star, for we have made progress. It is God who gives His gifts and graces to whom He will to complete His work." When I finished my training, I would be able to tell people about the afterlife. Without them revealing their problems to me, I would have the knowledge to help them.

I learned another important lesson one night through a dream. I was looking at a sheep, and it turned into a man. The man was very small and of a different nationality. He started to give me advice on some of my own personal issues. In my dream, I was thinking how fortunate I was to receive this help. After I woke up, St.Michael came and said that God can come through in many ways, in different forms, and through different kinds of people. He said we should never discriminate, but stay open to all and give all a chance to speak. He said how important it is to treat all people equally. In another dream, I was out shopping and came across a man with polyester pants, plastic shoes and a shirt that barely buttoned over his rotund belly. My carriage bumped into his and he started speaking to me. Suddenly, I realized it was my angel's voice! I said, "My angel, is that you? I did not know you were a shopper, here!" He said, "Yes, My Little Star, it is I, and let this be a lesson to you. For I know how much you love me, but you would never expect me to have this appearance, would you? It does not matter what one looks like. We must love all. For you see, if I had come to you like this, on the onset, you would not have looked at me or given me the time of day."

Then I heard Mary and she explained to me again how God made us all differently and how He loves all of us for who and what we are. She said I would be working with the poor and wealthy alike. It would not make a difference who they were in earthly terms. It was important for me to love and help them along their earthly journey. They were trying to teach me never to judge by one's appearance or by what they have or have not. For the person who looks like they have the least, may be the one that brings the most love and joy into our life. I slowly, started to comprehend more of Heaven's ways as opposed to man's ways. Not long after this, while doing some mundane household chores, I suddenly heard Jesus, "One makes My Heart proud by never failing another." As was His custom, He then sent the angel, "Say this 'My Little Star', 'My heart can only love!' "

I began to feel a sense of encouragement. It is really hard to explain this training, even though I have tried many times. Often, it felt like a flurry of Heavenly messages that built upon a common theme, and other times, it felt like a tornado of information. I was grateful for Fr. Aniello's suggestion to start a journal, because the messages I received were often brief, but spoke volumes. They had a deeper meaning each time I reflected upon them. I would bring my journal to our meetings and Fr. Aniello would help me to decipher what they meant.

The following are a few stories from my journal that will illustrate my experiences during this time period:

"This is My Gift to you"
It was my birthday, September of 1999. I received a vision of Jesus with His two hands behind His back. He

said, "Pick a hand." I picked His right hand. In it was a box. He unwrapped the box and inside was a heart, just like a beautiful valentine. He said, "This is My gift to you. It is all My love for you." He then showed me a vision of an open field of flowers. He said, "Occasionally I stop to pick one, to hold and enjoy." As He showed me a single flower in His hand He said, "This is you; your stem is so strong, I can barely hold you at times, because you want to grow so quickly. It is time now to let other people enter your life, you must show others." He understood my eagerness to have the training over with, and then to go out and do His work. He wanted me to slow down and absorb these teachings and apply them to my life before I could progress.

<u>"This is for your eternal life."</u>
I was praying to Jesus one night and as always I would feel totally at peace. I asked, "Jesus, can I go with You? I do not want to stay here anymore. I want to go with You." He said, "It would be unfair of Me to take you now. You will remain on earth and help others." During this time, the Blessed Mother said, "At times I have a hard time watching your training." St.Michael followed up by saying, "This is for your eternal life. You must have full desire to do our duties. You must love all and provide help to all. You are to help whoever it is we send to you with kindness and love." He made it very clear that Jesus would not give me this gift until I was totally willing and had full trust in God. He encouraged me by saying how well I was progressing, and that He would give me a break from the rigorous training and allow me to learn from a different

angle. It would happen through conversations about world economy and events. He told me how God saw the importance of man cooperating and helping one another. He used the expression, 'White collar and blue collar helping one another.' He said eventually people would help each other, work together and love each other.

"Three Tulips"
One day the Blessed Mother showed me a vision of three tulips: yellow, purple, and red. Just a vision, no message. Fr. Aniello told me to keep this in my journal because it could be some type of message for the future. Two weeks later, I saw on tv the same exact picture of three tulips, the exact colors, in the same order, yellow, purple and red. It happened to be a program about prophets and prophecy, true prophets and false prophets, and I knew I was supposed to watch it. After this program, it was easier for me to discern the difference. I learned that God chooses a prophet to teach and deliver His truth. The information that God gives is to be used for the benefit of others.

One day I noticed the water in the shower looked like crystals and my hands no longer looked like my hands. I heard the Blessed Mother say, "You will be a true prophet. Your hands will help my people who are in need." I was in the process of learning that I would be helping all who were sent to me regardless of who they were. It was important for me to be there to love and help them along their earthly journey. She concluded by saying, "Your life will be for all." Jesus taught me the importance of order, the importance of family, how forgiveness is crucial, and how we are to love one another.

"Lighten your Load"

"Has anyone ever made it, Jesus?" He replied, "Yes! My Mother." I realized that Jesus was asking all of us to see His Mother as a role model. He was encouraging all of us to follow her example and not give up. He said if He didn't know I would make it, He would not have chosen me. I asked Jesus if I would have healing gifts, and He said I would have to earn this through full and complete faith. I asked Him when I would have full faith, and He promised that it would be soon. I asked Him why He could not just give me healing gifts as I felt that I was ready. He showed me that I was still struggling between the material and spiritual world. He reassured me I must put God first, then others, and then myself, in that order. Jesus then showed me a wooden cart, with the wheels turning inward from the weight of the load. He said, "Lighten your load and then I will pull you to the top." He was showing me through this vision that I was still clinging so tightly to my house, my car, and my financial security, that I was weighing myself down. All of these earthly things meant nothing and I was to totally trust in Him alone. He reminded me that I'd been chosen by His Father to work for their world. "Remember, your life is mine; My life is yours."

January 2000

After Christmas, I felt the pull towards materialism and working again. I yearned to be around people again and

back into real estate. I was good at it and I was growing weary of what I perceived as my slow progression in
Heaven's training program. Why couldn't I still do real
estate and work for Heaven at the same time? I had really
loved my career and I still occasionally questioned why I
needed to give it up.

"Bricks and Stones"

On my way home I noticed a new mall being built. I so
wanted to be involved in a project like that. Later I received
a vision of a bulldozer in the middle of a field, engulfed in
flames. The vision remained for about two minutes. After
that, the Blessed Mother said to me, "There are a lot more
important and better things than this in life. Try to let go
of this. There are things more important than bricks and
stones. These are earth's ways. Try to let go of this, for
even if you were to have this, you could not take it with
you when you come home. Your real treasures are in my
world. So many of my children get stuck. They cannot see
beyond this." I then heard Jesus say, "You must have the
desire to build for your eternal life!" This was a good lesson for me to learn and through the years I've passed it
on. We can get to Heaven from anywhere on earth if we
put God first.

Jesus reminded me the following day that He had a better plan for me. He said life without love was not their
way and that I needed to prepare myself for His work
by having more trust, in what was ahead for me. He explained how short life is here in comparison to eternal life.
Jesus stressed that unless I got my impatience and short

temperedness under control, He would not be able to give me the knowledge I needed for this mission. It would only bring harm.

The next day the Blessed Mother told me gently that I still needed more training and more time with them. I became agitated because I thought I had already accomplished this. Out of frustration, I blurted out, "I don't want to do this anymore!" I was feeling sorry for myself and I seemed to forget who I was speaking to . . My voice became louder and more agitated. She waited until I was finished complaining. Finally she patiently responded, "My love, your strengths are more than what they should be." She showed me how out of control I was and how in control she was. "You are humble. Now you need to have control of yourself. You can always count on me. Your anger is harming you," she said. After she left I called for St.Michael, immediately he said, "You can stay down in despair or you can stand up and pray." I was so frustrated at this point. I asked if he could increase my knowledge. Without skipping a beat he replied, "You are asking God for ten dollars and right now you are a fifty cent pen! A fifty cent pen doesn't write very well so therefore we must be patient and continue on with our training!" He put me in my place fast, emphasizing how much work I still had to do within myself.

Just at that moment, something inside me changed and I had a clearer understanding of the process of these Heavenly lessons and a greater compassion for my fellow man.

In the distance I heard my angel St.Michael saying, "Lord, Lord, her walk on earth is long, before the truths happen." The Blessed Mother then told me that things would be quiet for a while. "Take a break." After she spoke these words, I did not hear from them for several months.

CHAPTER 10

"You know of my Son now, and He has your heart."

The silence really caught me off guard. I was so sorry that my outburst had caused such heavenly silence, but it gave me time to think. Through my spiritual direction and reflecting, I realized it was the familiarity and drive towards my former life that was distracting me. I was still unsure of myself with the work that Jesus had planned for me, partly because I had to work on changing myself and my negative traits. But it was also because there was this bigger unknown future ahead of me. Where would I be in 10 years? What would I be doing and would I enjoy it?

After much reflection and prayer I realized that I needed the same desire for God's plan as I did for my real estate career, (even though I did not know what His plan was.) I knew I wasn't trusting enough in the great mission He was calling me to. He saved me from Satan, physically healed me, gave me this incredible angel to guide and speak to me, and even allowed me to speak to His most gentle Mother! Heaven wanted me to reflect on all that had been granted to me. In a flash I understood that my current pace appeared slow by human standards, but it was a thousand times more rigorous and challenging than chasing real estate. God gave us all the great gift of free will but I knew I had to choose His plan.

It finally occurred to me that I didn't need to know what it was or where I was going specifically, because it was surely going to be a greater future than I could imagine. It was why God created me in the first place. I was heading towards my mission and Jesus wanted me to desire it. This thought started to energize me with the anticipation of finding out what it might be. I prayed to Jesus to increase my faith and trust in Him as I accepted the future that lay ahead. After my rest from training, I heard Jesus say, "My desire is for you to continue on... for I am back." Then I was given the privilege of seeing a bright vivid color vision of Jesus. He was wearing a golden robe with white cuffs and majestically standing in a shimmering pool of water looking up to Heaven. Behind Him was a dazzling waterfall. The water appeared as brilliant crystals and all the colors in the vision were radiantly amplified. After the vision ended I heard His voice again, "No harm will come to you, for I will turn all harm away." I began thanking Him for coming back to me and promised Him my loyalty, I was so grateful! I excitedly asked, "When the angel first came to me, I had full knowledge. I knew everything! Will I always have that knowledge?" Jesus, ever so patiently said, "You will have the knowledge you will need to complete the mission I put before you. The more you love, the more clarity you will have. I will send you others and you will send them back to Me over and over again."

The Blessed Mother said, "You will make it. You are asking for more knowledge. When this is given, it is important that you hold on to me." The way she said it almost sounded like a warning and I wondered why. What could be so bad about having more knowledge? That's when I heard Michael's voice warn, "More power... people will say things... you will have to control yourself. The more your gifts increase, the more you can expect criticism." He told me that, while listening to my story, many would see this as a foreign language and not understand. The Blessed Mother went on to say, "You will have people test you. When this happens your angel will tell you. Our Father gets very frustrated when He sees this. Remember, stay focused on me. Focus on my heart, focus on my love. I will know who is sitting in front of you; you will not. Only give the person the information that is given to you. Most importantly, do not get ahead of me, your angel or Jesus. Listen carefully and only repeat to that person what is told to you. Never add your own information; it will most likely be wrong. Work on your manner, work on your poise. People will question how you are transmitting this information. They will know it is from Heaven by the fruit of your labor. Do not get upset, do not push. At times, you will not tell them of your gifts. You will just say that you are there to help. There are times when it is not important for the individual to know that you are speaking to us. What matters is the task being completed. Our way is to let others receive what you have been given... our gifts."

Shortly thereafter, the Blessed Mother told me, "Your work cannot begin until my Son is finished with your training… blessed are the fruits of your work." I was sure that the number one fruit she was referring to was patience. She then said that I was being transformed, which gave me a new feeling of hope, and made me want to emulate her all the more. On different occasions, I would hear my angel say, "Good things come to those who love. If you believe, if you love, good things will come. You are my light, ever so bright and I will always fight, for things of the light. You, My Little Star are ever so bright." My angel taught me that I could not control the lives of others, only my own. He told me that I would have strength and I would stay strong.

June 10 2000

I heard Jesus above me, speaking of His world. I felt His presence, an indescribable sensation of peace. He then kissed me on my right cheek. When he left, St.Michael came and he was very joyful! He told me that Jesus very rarely does this, that I did not have any idea how privileged I was to have been kissed on the cheek by Jesus. Here I was an ordinary person and suddenly I was asked by God to do His work. I felt so humbled and honored. This gave me great confidence and reassurance to continue on.

The Blessed Mother said, "Before Our Lord sends you His gifts, you will have to let go of all earth's boundaries and relinquish all your control. You must trust that Jesus can replenish. You must let go and let Jesus take the boat.

Think back to when you were a little girl talking to your mother while she ironed. You would say to her you were not going to be poor when you grew up," she continued. "You will do our work. You will have what it is you asked for. This gift is rarely given. The purpose of this gift is to have our people notice Our Lord. Your heart has grown more than you will ever know. I can give you our love. Our love is better than anything you can obtain on earth." She was telling me that I would become rich in spirit through their love and because of this, experience a much deeper love for others.

The angel continued to help me work on myself. "We are going to have poise and be outgoing and vibrant. Poise means self control," St. Michael said. "Before you believe in me, you must believe in yourself and then you must believe that I am with you. Also, believe that I will never fail you. Belief means knowing I am going to be here for you. Belief is so important. Our belief is what attracts what we are asking for!" Feeling this truth in my heart first, and then hearing those exact words from him gave me a confirmation of friendship, loyalty, and trust that made me love St. Michael in a special new way. This new surge of confident joy pierced my heart and suddenly, not only was St. Michael my mentor; he was also family. I loved him on a whole new level. Knowing that he loved me and would guide me gave me great courage and increased my faith. He had been with me for so long and had seen me through so many low points. I didn't fear what this new life would be like; now I couldn't wait to conquer our next new adventure.

That week I heard Jesus say, "The Heavens are yours; miracle working gifts. When My Mother is ready, she will call for you. Continue on loving. Travel light, people will want our time, but we do not want people's money." Jesus was telling me to freely give my gift to help others. It seemed Jesus was speaking to me as if He had confidence in me and I was ready for His plan. In His unique way of speaking, He was giving me instructions while giving me instant recall to these exact words so that I could retrieve them later when I needed His guidance. I was so grateful to have passed through this part of the trial, but still nervous to be heading into the unknown. I recalled the previous lesson about having faith in their plan, even though I did not have a blue print. Deep in my soul I knew, that putting my trust in God was all that I needed to do, to succeed, and I was now determined to be strong and resist the temptation of being afraid of the unknown.

I fell asleep and had a dream. I was in the kitchen of a restaurant, looking at an unshaven man. His clothes were dirty and he was swearing. He had a hot temper and a bad attitude, but he appeared to be working hard. In the next segment of the dream, we were in the lounge of the same restaurant. There was the same man, with his hair cut, clean and nicely dressed. He was playing a piano beautifully. He was calm and very loving. People were gathered around the piano, speaking of how well he played and how soothing his music was. Jesus was telling me that He can transform us for the better if we choose Him. We can become better versions of ourselves if we stand back, listen and trust in Him.

I was starting to understand this, and more importantly, I was starting to desire it. I told myself that I could do this for Him. I would trust Him to transform me into a better person. When the dream ended, I received a message from Jesus. "The miracle is this. What new love can do, if you let yourself be guided through." Jesus was showing me that he can transform us for the better, if we choose Him. Next, I saw Jesus' hands putting coins in a piggy bank. He said, "Every time you do a good deed, a coin goes into your bank." Little did I know, down the road when I began His work, I would ask Him for favors for others to be healed. I worked very hard to collect these coins in my bank. When I needed them for someone who was in need of healing or very sick, I would pray to Jesus to use the coins in order to lift the disease from the individual, if it was His Will. Many times, I would see the miracle happen right before my eyes!

Now I started practicing in the real world, taking baby steps. Heaven was going to give me a lot of opportunities to learn patience and hold my tongue. I went to a gas station, and as I was putting the nozzle in my car, a man with a plastic container walked up to me, grabbed the nozzle out of my hand and started to fill his container! I heard St Michael say, "My Little Star, do nothing." I was trying to be obedient, so I stood there in silence. When he finished, I pumped my gas. When I got back in my car my angel said, "Good, you passed this test." Next I went into a shop for coffee. Standing in a long line, a woman pushed her way ahead of me. I said, "Excuse me, you just cut in front of me. Please go to the back of the line." The woman started to shout at me and I shouted back. When I got in the car, I asked St. Michael what he thought. He said, "You are weak, very weak. A strong person would have said nothing." I had to repeat these lessons over and over until I perfected them.

One day I said to the Blessed Mother that I would like this and I would like that. I detailed every desire and wish, endlessly babbling. When I paused, she simply said, "Your wants and desires are more than you need. This won't help you. I will help you." It never ceases to amaze me how Heaven speaks with so few words which mean so much.

That same month I was invited to a prayer meeting with a group of nuns. I tried to speak to one of the nuns about the mystical things I'd been experiencing. She was very harsh with me and was not understanding of my gift. I avoided her the rest of the evening. At the end of the night, there was a crowd of people surrounding her. I walked up to her and sarcastically said, "Sister, thank you for your warm welcome." When I got into my car, I immediately heard the Blessed Mother say, "Next time, say this in silence." I then heard Jesus.... "She does not know any better." Again, Jesus, the Blessed Mother and St. Michael were teaching me their gentleness and kindness towards others.

One hot August day, Paulette and I decided to have a cook-out at my home. We invited Fr. Aniello and several others. I stepped out onto the deck and was overcome by the most horrible odor imaginable. I walked around the second story deck, looking down, to see if there was a dead animal nearby. Paulette had gone to the ground level to look and found nothing either. She called to me, "Maureen, why don't you ask the angel where the dead animal is?" I shrugged my shoulders, as I wasn't sure Heaven would concern itself with my attempting to find a dead animal, but I decided to give it a try. Suddenly, I heard St.Michael's voice! He said, "Have her follow your direction." He pointed into a heavily wooded area. The trees and brush were so thick, Paulette had difficulty making her way there. He said, "Walk this way." I repeated this to her and she was led to a big maple tree. That's when I heard her scream! There it was, a big, bloated possum decaying in the heat. The stench was unbearable. She scooped it up with a pitchfork and threw it further up in the woods. After this ordeal, I thanked my angel for all of his help. He told me he had assisted me so I would continue to build up my trust in him. By the time we had our dinner on the deck, the smell had completely dissipated and I remember Fr. Aniello's jovial laughter as he heard the story!

July 31, 2000
I was getting ready one morning and I felt an acute stinging in my right hand. I looked down and there was a clear precise slice across the palm, almost like a razor blade had cut it. I knew I had done nothing to cut my hand this badly. Flinching, I closed my hand. It was burning and stinging. When I opened my hand to run cold water over it, I literally saw the cut healing itself right before my eyes! I then heard Jesus' voice, "This is Me. This is My love for you, these are My gifts."

That same week I decided to reorganize my basement. A friend of mine offered to help me and we worked the entire day. We had been lifting boxes and I started to feel exhausted. My friend decided to stay over. At 2:00 AM, I was awakened with excruciating pain in my lower back and I also noticed my left leg was numb. I had a flashback of the angel telling me to avoid heavy lifting. The pain was so unbearable, I was afraid to move a muscle. I was trembling and called out to my friend who was in a room down the hall. Being a nurse, she realized the seriousness of my pain and suggested we call an ambulance. She tried to move my legs gently but the pain was too intense. In desperation, I cried out for Jesus to help me. Instantly, I heard His voice and a sensation of peace flooded my soul. He told me I would be okay. As He was speaking to me, He levitated me up horizontally, off the bed, then slowly turned me vertically and placed me against the wall with my feet touching the floor. He then said, "Walk." Needless to say, my friend could not believe what she had just witnessed and just stood there speechless. We then slowly walked to the kitchen and she suggested I take an anti inflammatory pill. I heard Jesus say, "Follow her instructions." After this the pain subsided; I was able to walk comfortably back to my bedroom and get some rest.

Jesus was showing me His miracle working powers.

August 16, 2000
I started to see things from a different perspective and how mundane life sometimes seems to be. I noticed people loosing their tempers in rush hour traffic or people impatiently standing in line at the grocery store. Everyone

looked tired and restless having to get through these everyday tasks. As I became more attentive, so did my understanding of people. I could see they were not aware God was offering special blessings in each moment. Every moment was a gift, even if it seemed like a burden. There were so many opportunities for people to transform the world with love and prayer.

St.Michael went on to tell me the four things most people want are money, love, control and power. Before you obtain money, it is important you obtain love first. In order to obtain control, you must have control. Many people let money control them when in fact they must control the money. Most people feel that money, control and love give them power. This is not God's definition of power. The Blessed Mother said, "So many people's wills are so strong for money. At times, I have a hard time holding on to them." I then heard Jesus, "If a woman knelt in front of you and said 'I love you. Will you help me?' Would you help her?" I eagerly replied, "Yes Jesus, I would." Jesus replied, "Then know, I will help you." I asked what would happen if I conformed to everything God was asking of me. Mary replied, "Then you would be in control. Most of my children turn away from me. They do not want to hear what I say. You cannot have earthly things in Heaven. You will find that material gain has never helped anyone. Expecting material gain from another never works. Jesus does not want material things controlling us." The Blessed Mother gave me another example. If I were to take a million dollars in return for giving someone information, I would have to answer to God for this when I died. God always looks at one's intentions. She went on; "The purpose of this gift given to you is to have people notice Our Lord and be fully complete without money. You will accomplish this with love." She was affirming that this gift was not about me but was a vehicle to bring souls back to God. It was sinking in that God sees our value in who we are, not in what we have. We must trust God who will love, guide and protect us on our journey.

The Blessed Mother told me that they would never harm one to help another. Jesus said, "Finish developing. My Mother has plans for you. I will show you the way." I told the Blessed Mother that after three years, I felt my progress was slow. She replied, "What will help you accomplish this is prayer and love. In our world development means spending quiet time and learning with us in Heaven. Stay close to me. The plan is to help you first, then our people with our knowledge through time. You will then tell people of our world. Remember, I always want you to stay small." She went on to tell me that self importance doesn't matter. God looks at how much an individual loved, how much they gave, how much compassion they had." She continued ever so gently, "You know of my Son now, and He has your heart. Our Father wants you to have a way," referring to me having a way home to Heaven. She said, "My heart wants nothing more than to have your heart come home. My heart is with you every step." Conversations like this went on for months and I was finally fully understanding the work Heaven wanted me to do.

I felt St.Michael smiling as he said, "Never doubt. Helping people will bring you fulfillment. Fulfillment means work. Work with me. Make Jesus proud by never failing another." This time, his encouragement seemed to ring true and I felt a deepening sense of emotion in my heart. I heard him lovingly whisper, "The Blessed Mother has built you. Love Our Father and trust in Jesus."

I now knew that the love coming from Heaven was unconditional and all encompassing, incomparable to our concept of love here on earth. Love here is based on emotions and feelings that may change from day to day. God's love is merciful, undying and unconditional. God is Love.

And I knew it was just that simple.

CHAPTER 11

"So as fall comes before winter, dark comes before light, so does prayer come before miracles"

At times I had wavered. I felt I had one foot on earth and one foot in Heaven. I was trying to make these two worlds coexist in my life. I knew, deep down in my heart, that there was nothing greater than service to God, but I was so tired. I had the desire and drive to do God's will, but I needed to find a way to refresh myself. Suddenly, Our Blessed Mother came to me and simply said, "St. Bernadette, study her. Learn of her life when she was on earth."

Excited to have a different assignment, I talked to Paulette and she immediately went out and bought a book on St. Bernadette. Paulette knew that I was not an avid reader so she read the book and then told me the entire story. I learned that Bernadette was French and had several apparitions of the Blessed Virgin Mary at Lourdes, France. Lourdes became a major pilgrimage site for miraculous healings. Bernadette came from an extremely poor family and could not read or write. In a town full of nobles, she was considered a nobody. In God's eyes she was a valuable soul. The Blessed Mother told St. Bernadette, "I cannot promise you happiness in this world but I can in the next." I realized that this work for God would be tiring but if I stayed the course I would receive my merit in Heaven. It had been a long week with many revelations. I sat down in my favorite chair to relax. Softly, Mary said she had someone with her who would like to speak to me. I asked who it was and suddenly I heard St. Bernadette! She simply said, "I have a message for you. Know that you have been watched over." That is all she said and then she was gone. Wow! God actually allowed me to hear from a saint that I had just learned about! And she was watching over me. It was mind boggling. I kept working on improving myself, trying to stay humble and small. The next day I had a problem with my fax machine. It appeared to be jammed. When I opened it up, I discovered a St. Bernadette medal. Immediately I heard St.Michael say, "This is a message for you. The Blessed Mother sent this so you wouldn't forget this girl put herself aside for others." This was just the encouragement I needed to reach the goal I had been training for.

Heaven asked me to learn of Elijah the Prophet along with St. Bernadette. Now it was all coming together in my head and I understood why. They were helping me grasp what was happening to me. They wanted me to see that God has chosen many different kinds of people throughout the centuries from various backgrounds to do His work here on earth, to teach and show others that God exists.

I worried sometimes that I spent more time with Mary than Jesus. I was so drawn to her gentleness and compassion. She said, "Time spent with me is time spent with my Son. Time spent with my Son is the same as time spent with me or Our Father." When I prayed the rosary, my hands would get extremely hot. The Blessed Mother would often say, "We are all as One. Love others more. You have the gifts now to help people. The more people you help, the more you will be helped." She continued on with her motherly lessons saying, "Make my heart warm, tell our people of my heart and my love. Life is not easy and gifts, when given by Our Father, are not easy. It requires letting go of earth's boundaries, prayer, and focus on your willingness to want all of this. For our kingdom must come first, then the knowledge will be given."

Sometimes I would not understand a word in one of Heaven's messages.

"Behold, My Father denies those that depend on mammon and not on His love." Mammon? What was that? I called Fr. Aniello to help me with this message. He told me that "mammon" was a term that Jesus used meaning riches or material wealth. Now I understood the message completely.

Jesus gave me the analogy of a sharpened pencil that writes nicely, meaning His instrument. "When I need to write, I pick up the pencil and write," He said, "When I am through writing, I put it back down. I would rather use a sharp instrument for a shorter period of time, than use a dull instrument. My pen only writes with love." He was showing me that once I was "sharpened," he would use me when He needed. Jesus also told me that He would not display His plan to me. I was to take each day as it was to come. "You have become my instrument. Blessed are those who see Me. I called you and you came forth. You must depend on Me." Jesus said. "In our world, an apprentice will be paid the same as a craftsman," Mary said. "My Son depends on your heart and loves all His children equally."

As my training was coming to a close, the Blessed Mother was preparing me for situations I would encounter in 'the field.' She explained that sometimes, I would not understand the message she would have for someone, and that it did not matter. I did not need to know, and if I did know, it might be a disadvantage to that person. All I needed to do was to repeat the message for that person verbatim.

The Blessed Mother said, "You find my words harsh." (meaning she did not want me to speak of or rely on earthly things) I will never forget what you have done. People won't know who you are at times and many times you will go in silence. Do not say my name, just say, 'I will try to help.' They will know you are talking to someone. When I was on earth people thought I was more than, because I was chosen. I endured pain. My heart is with you every step of the way. Depend on me. I want nothing more than for you to succeed. This work needs my spirit. The time is near. So many are of self indulgence. Our Father only picks flowers from the garden of love. There are not enough flowers. Many are coming in fear because they see the (state of) world." Then I heard St. Michael say, "She is gathering her flowers now for her army. She will be on the battlefield. This will be." He was explaining that she is on the battlefield in the spiritual realm. Combating evil, she is battling to convert souls and bring them to God.

She told me, "So as fall comes before winter, dark comes before light, so does prayer come before miracles. This life is filled with darkness. You will open the sky and fill it with love and light. You have strength. Your heart needs to love more, so you can be open to bring love forth to our people. You have many gifts, but the greatest gift is bringing the fruits of our love to all who can see. For soon the days will end and for those who remain, the world will be anew. For those who cannot see, only darkness will remain. You have much work. All your gifts will excel when your heart is filled with love. Our world (meaning earth) sits in darkness. When your heart is filled, you will hear all. You will have angels, you will have the Holy Spirit, you will have the greatest protector (meaning St.Michael the Archangel). He has always been yours. Trust your abilities. All of your desires you will obtain. Trust us." The words were so powerful and were resounding in my heart; now I would apply them to every facet of my life.

CHAPTER 12

"It is time now for a miracle."

After three years of training about love, kindness, and changing myself, my work was about to begin. I was given beautiful gifts by God the Father and my work began with St. Michael, to help others who were in need. I was helping people, one at a time, usually by phone. People would ask me all sorts of questions pertaining to their health, difficult relationships, loss of a job or wanting to know if their loved ones were in Heaven. Often times, St.Michael would advise me and tell me what to say, and I would relay his message exactly as I heard it. Sometimes, Mary or Jesus Himself would give a short answer, and even if I did not think it had much information, it was always exactly what the person needed to hear. Just a short message or a small comment meant a lot to the person. There were times that Heaven was silent. At first, I thought I was not listening correctly, but I learned that there was a reason for this. It was frustrating for the person, but I assured them that Heaven always knew what information was best for them and they were still very much loved.

As word traveled and one person would tell another about the 'lady who talks to Heaven,' more calls would come in asking for Heavenly advice. The phone calls would start at 7:00 AM and some days I would find myself still taking calls at 7:00 PM. I was starting to realize how much stamina this was going to take and what a great responsibility it was to be doing Jesus' work. There were so many people in pain and so many lost souls that were hungry for God, even if they did not realize it at the time.

Once I gained experience relaying Heaven's messages, Fr. Aniello invited me to join his healing services. It was only a short time before people learned of my gift and the angel St. Michael and flocked to sit with me. All would leave having been enlightened. A woman asked me to ask St. Michael what was the highest form of prayer. This time the Blessed Mother came to me and simply said, "Love." Then I sat with two women, one had lost her son and the other had lost her husband. They were looking for confirmation that their loved ones were safe on the other side. St.Michael said "Have trust and faith." He then went on giving them guidance to help them with their emotional problems and teach them how they could overcome these obstacles. One of the women was staying home and mourning the loss of her son all day, something her son would not want, and St. Michael urged her to go forward and live a full life, this being what her son would want. Both women asked if I was familiar with a certain male television personality who supposedly could tell people about their deceased loves ones. They would ask if I could get the same type of information that he allegedly received, (for example peculiar traits of the deceased, such as the woman's son liked smoking filterless cigarettes or the other woman's husband liked kayaking.) I called for St.Michael about this but received no answer. He only referred back to the women's emotional state and said this was much more important for their well being. When I went home that night, I prayed to Jesus and asked why I was not receiving the type of information that some people were looking for (confirmation of what the deceased person did or did not do while on earth). Jesus replied, "My plane is where it should not be, My plane is lost, My plane is out of it's flight pattern. More growth... formation. I want you to fly the jet." This was Jesus' way of telling me that this was not the path He wanted me on, and not the way in which He wanted me to use the gift He had given me to help people.

Fr. Aniello and I would meet often as we discussed my experiences; his guidance was important. One time he asked "Maureen, please, would you ask St. Michael how many times will God show us the truth after we die. The truth meaning God's plan of salvation in Jesus and a clear judgement of our personal responsibility for our actions. I closed my eyes and silently asked the angel and this was his reply, "God will continue to show us until we have a full understanding of the truth about ourselves and the plan of salvation in Jesus, so that we can exercise our freedom with full knowledge and accept or refuse his plan."

Soon, he felt that I was up to the task of accompanying him when he visited a woman who was under attack by

Satan. He knew that I had reached the point where I had no fear of Satan, and was fully grounded in my faith. It was important to me to know he had enough confidence in me to do this work with him. I looked up to him as a true friend and father figure. When we arrived, I immediately felt an evil presence in the woman's home. She was middle-aged, married and financially well off. Fr. Aniello prayed over her and blessed her along with the house. He counseled her about things she needed to change in her life. Over the next year, Fr. Aniello and I worked closely with her, trying to help her rebuke and release this evil presence from within herself. Unfortunately, sometimes a person who has been delivered from the bondage of Satan sometimes allows him back into their life. She continued to communicate with Satan, and therefore she was not freed from his oppressive influence. This was her choice by her own free will. I continued to make many visits with Fr. Aniello to various people with similar demonic problems.

Satan wants us to believe that he is an angel of light with our best interests as his goal, but he is the 'father of lies'. He will feed a person fruitless information or give them confirmation of something in the past, just to gain their confidence. Satan will many times give 90% correct information and 10% incorrect information. He gives enough correct information to sound credible and make you believe you are hearing an angel. But the incorrect information will be enough to ultimately misguide and deceive you and be your demise. The more one tries to discern, the more clever Satan becomes. Satan can take on the form of anyone or anything to deceive us. It's always important to remember that Satan hates humanity and his mission is to prevent us from achieving eternal life with God. If he does not succeed at this he will try to influence us negatively and rob us of peace, love and joy.

One day, Fr. Aniello called me to meet with another woman who had been under attack by Satan. As we were praying over her, I sensed Satan was present. The woman's voice changed and Satan started speaking through her, growling, "You stupid fool, you stupid fool, you don't know what you are doing!" Father and I continued praying and finally Jesus expelled the demon. The woman went on her way, only to return several months later with the same problem. She would resume communicating with Satan and we would have to start all over again. I was often perplexed that the temptation was still there for people to return to Satan and not stay with Jesus. That night Fr. Aniello woke up in the middle of the night being choked by Satan. He called for Jesus and immediately was released. This was demonic retaliation for his work that day.

On another occaision I had just retired for the evening when I heard heavy foot steps coming down the hall towards my bedroom. The sinister dark figure of Satan entered the room and put a revolver to my head. I felt a quick adrenaline rush of fear and then the cold steel of the gun barrel pressing hard into my temple. I collected myself and did what I was trained to do, that is, I called quietly for Jesus, Our Father and the Blessed Mother to rescue me. It seemed the more I prayed, the harder the gun was pushed into my head. Finally the pain became so unbearable I yelled out "Go ahead, pull the trigger, because you know you can't!" Precisely at that moment Satan vanished. Even though Our Father had to permit this attack, I had full faith and a 'knowing' that Satan was not allowed to pull the trigger. It's imperative that we always pray for guidance and protection with full faith and trust in Our Father that He will never allow Satan to bring harm to us. I was beginning to see that Satan had his own agenda and often used terror tactics to interfere with someone who opposed him, or tried to leave him.

Many believe that if someone is involved with or feels they are possessed by Satan then Satan has the ability to enter their soul. This is absolutely false. A person would have to give Satan permission to take possession of their soul in order for this to happen. Remember, we have free will. If no permission is given then there can be no full possession. Many times a person may think they are possessed when it is actually mental illness or drug related. A very small percentage of these people are actually possessed. Any other type of paranormal activity coming from evil is an exterior attack, meaning Satan is attacking the person from the outside. A few examples, lights flickering, electronic malfunctions, banging noises, scratches, hearing voices, etc. There is no reason to be afraid of this. The only way he can harm you is self-harm; which is one's own fear. The more fearful we become, the more the activity will accelerate. Many people I have sat with have experienced external paranormal activity in their homes and they have had no involvement with Satan, new age teachings, tarot cards, ouija boards, fortunetellers etc. which attracts demonic activity. I have seen through the years that God will sometimes permit this activity to draw a soul back to Him. Some of the problems that attract this activity are unforgiveness towards God, a person who has turned away from God, or a person who does not recognize or know God. Other common causes are unforgiveness toward someone who has caused them harm, or someone caught in and controlled by the material world. Many times if they turn back to God, with full faith, trust and belief this activity usually diminishes or stops.

I soon started sitting with large groups of people at healing services, listening to hundreds of questions and obtaining answers from Heaven. It became very draining on me because it required the utmost concentration. I had to listen to the person... wait for St.Michael...concentrate... listen to his answer...then repeat it word for word to the person. This would also limit how many people I could sit with at a time. I prayed to the Blessed Mother and Jesus, asking if there was a better way to assist more people. The Blessed Mother responded, "Yes. The next time you sit with a large group, I will show you." A few days later I had a group of fifty or so waiting for me. I had a terrible sinus infection and a fever. I asked the Blessed Mother how I would get through this, when I heard her say, "Go, and know that you will just have the knowledge." When I walked into the room, I was astounded! I had been given the knowledge to answer every person's questions! I went to each individual and explained that I did not need to hear their question, that I had answers for them already! The people were amazed. I was so happy to see how fast I could help so many people this way. It took about one quarter of the time it normally took. This method worked very well and all the information was completely accurate, so naturally I began to ask the Blessed Mother and Jesus for this knowledge whenever I would be working with a larger group.

One of the most common questions I am asked is "What am I supposed to be doing for Jesus? What does He want me to do?" I prayed about this and the Blessed Mother answered by saying "Just surrender and be willing." If we submit, Jesus will put in our path the direction we are to take. It is up to us whether to choose and accept what He sends us.

February 28, 2001
One morning, I awoke to find my hand grasping the miraculous medal that I wear around my neck. The Blessed Mother came and wrapped her hand around mine, and gently whispered, "It is time now for a miracle."The next day, I called Fr. Aniello and told him what Mary had promised. He told me to write this down and wait to see how this would unfold.

"The Miracle"
The mother of my sister's friend was in the hospital and had gone into a coma from an autoimmune problem. She had been placed on life support. My sister seemed to think

the miracle was for her friend's mom. We went into ICU and while praying over this woman in the coma, I called for the Blessed Mother. She said, "This woman does not want to go 'home,' because her son does not want to let her go. Tell him that I want to wrap her in my arms and take her to my Heavens." I explained this to the woman's son. He put his head down and cried. "I do not want to let go of my mother, but tell the Blessed Mother, I trust in her and it's okay now. She can take her to Heaven." he said. She died peacefully several days later.

As my sister and I were leaving the hospital, a family approached us, asking me to pray over their mother. They explained that she was on life support and could not speak. It was one of those busy days for me and I was exhausted. I instantly had a flashback of Jesus telling me, "Sometimes when God calls, we have to give all." I knew Jesus would want me to go, so I agreed. She was surrounded by her husband and family members. Her husband told me that to communicate, she would blink two times for "no" and three times for "yes." I immediately called for St.Michael and I asked him how I could help this woman. Michael "stepped back" and said nothing. Suddenly, I saw the Blessed Mother come down (I saw her as a bright white light.) I heard her say, "We will speak to this woman now." She told me to tell this woman that she was aware she had prayed to her during her entire life, and that because of her deep faith, she was granted the privilege of witnessing a miracle. I relayed this to the family. They were all nodding their heads, 'Yes,' and the woman agreed by blinking three times. The Blessed Mother then said she would physically manifest herself to this woman. She said the woman did not want to let go because she had a message for each of her family members and could not speak. The Blessed Mother said, "Therefore, we will relay the message to each family member for her." I repeated word for word what the Blessed Mother was relaying to me. The Blessed Mother and I began to speak to each family member, giving them a message from their mother. As we spoke, the woman would blink for 'Yes'. Finally, we completed the circle of family members and got back to the woman. The Blessed Mother told me to share with the woman that she still needed to forgive her father who had abused her. After telling her the woman agreed by blinking. As I looked up, her husband said, "That's unbelievable. Who are you?" I explained to her husband that I was merely an instrument doing God's work. The Blessed Mother then went on to speak about this woman's mother, who had been an alcoholic. She continued telling me the woman must also forgive her mother, and I relayed this as well. Suddenly, I saw the brilliant light again and this time, I knew that this woman could see the Blessed Mother as well. "She's here! Can you see her?!" The woman was crying, blinking 'Yes!' She was crying so hard, she started choking. I noticed the Blessed Mother going up and leaving. The woman calmed down and stabilized. The Blessed Mother then returned. "She's here. Can you see her? Isn't she beautiful?" I exclaimed. She was crying and blinking her eyes for 'Yes'. Her family members were all around the bed in disbelief, saying what a privilege this was to be there for this miracle. This was the miracle the Blessed Mother had been speaking of, when she came into my room and held my hand.

Later that night I awoke again holding the miraculous medal with her hand gently wrapped around mine. I then heard the her say, "Blessed are those who see my love." Two days after this, the woman died peacefully.

"Can you see them? Jesus and Mary are here."

Several days later, I received a phone call from a family who wanted me to sit with their terminally ill father. I met him at the senior center. I called for the angel, but the Blessed Mother answered instead. She told me that this man had prayed to her all his life. The man confirmed this and asked me to ask the Blessed Mother when he was going to die. She would not answer this question, but reassured him that when the time was near, that she and her Son would come for him. Months later, I received a call informing me that this man was in the hospital and that the family was rotating their time with him. One night, no one in his family could be there. A nurse came in and was sitting with him. "Can you see them? Jesus and Mary are here," he said to the nurse. The nurse could not see them, but said she could feel their presence in the room. Shortly after, the man died. When the family got to the hospital, the nurse explained what had transpired. This was confirmation to the family that the Blessed Mother and Jesus came, as they promised, when the time was near to take their father home to Heaven. So many times, I have been with people in similar situations with a similar outcome. Jesus, the Blessed Mother or Michael would reassure them that they would be with their loved ones at death, and after the death, there would be confirmation that this happened.

"Tell her she needs Me."

Now my work pace was growing steadily every day. Many people were calling and Michael and I were sitting with them frequently. A woman called me who worked in the media. I told her a little bit about her childhood, her emotional problems, and confirmation of several other personal things. She was astounded and so intrigued that she came to the Shrine with me and met Fr. Aniello. She and I went into the chapel to pray. Jesus had a message for her: He said, "Tell her she needs Me." When I told her, she started crying and said, "He is right, Maureen, I do need Him." She had been through many hard times and these words of Jesus were just what she needed to hear. She was so relieved and continued to tell all her friends about the experience.

"God will not interfere with our free will."

A friend of a friend asked me to please come pray over his 19 year old nephew, who was gravely ill with a blood disease as well as autoimmune problems and could not fight off a deadly infection. I prayed to Jesus before I went to see him, and asked if He would heal him and He said, "Yes, all he needs to do is ask Me." I was so happy to tell this young boy the great news. The Blessed Mother informed me that this family was only looking for a miracle, that this was the only reason they were allowing me to sit with him. When I arrived, I sat with the young man and held his hand. He had strong faith in Jesus. I began telling him that he would be healed and that he only needed to ask Jesus. He would not make eye contact with me and kept looking down. I could not understand his reaction and why he was so unreceptive. Then he explained that he really did not want to be healed. He wanted to die so he could be with his deceased grandmother. He told me that his parents were so overly concerned with money, they had forgotten about him. All he could remember during his childhood was talk of money. His grandmother was the only one who spent time with him and took him places. He felt she was the only one who truly loved him. I stayed a while and prayed with him but I could not persuade him to ask to be healed. He died several months later. I was still learning that not everyone wants a healing and God will not interfere with our free will.

"Money is of No Consequence."

I received a call from a terminally ill woman. She mentioned that her sister was a famous actress. I agreed to meet with her the following day. She invited me in graciously and when I sat with her I called for Michael, but I could not get any information. I apologized and told her I was not hearing anything and that from time to time, this would happen. She told me matter of factly that her sister was a well known movie star, if she could be healed, there would be money and notoriety for me. I told her that God was the Healer, that I was just God's instrument, and money was of no consequence. I explained that it was up to God who was healed and if it was according to His plan. Just as I was about to leave, I heard Michael's voice and he gave her a little bit of information. As I tried to share it, she shut down and did not want to hear it. St.Michael told me to thank her for the visit and leave. When I got home that day, I was very bewildered. I called for the Blessed

Mother and asked, "Why didn't you tell me this before I went to this woman's house? Why didn't this woman get more information from St.Michael?" "When you go out to do our work, I know who is in front of you, you do not," she replied, "I know all about the individual. You do not. Just continue to follow God's will."

Several weeks later, I received a call from the same woman. She said the doctor had given her just two weeks to live, and asked if I would come back for a visit. I called Fr. Aniello and shared what had happened on the first visit and asked him to join me. Shortly after we arrived, St. Michael came and gave this woman the same short information she denied previously. Once again, the woman went into denial about what the angel was saying. Fr. Aniello immediately spoke up and said, "Stop, stop, this is not a game. The angel is never wrong." This got her attention and she began to listen. St.Michael pointed out that she had turned away from God several years earlier. Now Jesus was coming to save her soul before she died. After we spoke for a long time, she admitted to things she had done during her life that she regretted. St.Michael told her she had to forgive others who had harmed her. She agreed and then asked Fr. Aniello to hear her confession. As she grew closer to her death, she had fully repented and died peacefully.

At various times, I had offers that Heaven wanted me to decline. One was to do a radio talk show. I prayed to Jesus and asked if he wanted me to do this. He replied, "Not now. Now is not the time for this; there is something better ahead for you." Another offer was to provide information from St. Michael to solve cold cases. Again, I would go home and pray to the Blessed Mother and Jesus and ask if this was the direction they wanted me to take. Their response was "No, not now. More prayers, more help to others. There is something better ahead."

"The Bunnies"
I was doing some household chores one day and all of a sudden I heard Jesus' voice. He said, "Take these bunnies to the sick children in the hospital." That was all He said. I "saw" a stuffed toy bunny and I also "saw" the hospital I was to go to. I stopped what I was doing and called the hospital and asked for the children's ward. My call was transferred and I told a very nice nurse that I wanted to bring these stuffed bunnies to the children as gifts. She told me there were 28 children and said she would transfer me to "Katie" who was one of the volunteers who worked with these children. Katie thought it was a great idea and invited me to meet her when I had the toys. I immediately went shopping and found just the right bunnies, they were different colors, soft and cute. I met Katie at the hospital and we went from room to room giving the little bunnies to the children. Most were fighting cancer and taking strong treatments and I knew they were not feeling well, but still they were so grateful and appreciative. It was such a fulfilling day for me that I could give them each something special, make them smile and break up the monotony of their hospital stay.

"Do good and then disappear."
The Blessed Mother told me early in the year that many times I would help people without them being aware of

my gift. One night, a girlfriend and I were driving home in an ice storm. I was about a mile from home and I noticed something in the middle of the road. I heard St.Michael tell me to pull over. The roads were icy. Finally I realized there was a woman in the road, her face covered in blood. I didn't realize her car was further down the road, where she had collided with another car and had been thrown through the windshield. St.Michael quickly said, "Take your jacket and tend to her." My friend quickly called 911. I could barely walk on the slippery road. When I approached her, she seemed somewhat coherent. I knelt down and wrapped my jacket around her. "Reassure her that she is going to make it, that she will be okay," St.Michael said. The woman was shaking and bleeding from her head as I told her the good news. I could hear the sirens in the distance. The woman kept moaning, "Help me, help me." The woman was very afraid because she had no health insurance and was sharing this concern while we waited for help to arrive. The emergency vehicles arrived, but they initially went to the cars. I called the police to tell them we were up the road a bit. The ambulance finally found us and they took the woman to the hospital. Later that evening, I heard Jesus say, "Tonight you helped one of my sheep. Thank you." Several days later I heard the woman had survived and was doing fine."

"Do good and then disappear," I was once told. Disappear, because it is about Jesus, not me, the instrument. There were many times when I was sent to help anonymously. I was becoming a firm believer in God's providence. I was learning that He sends a person or people into one's life for a variety of reasons. It may be someone to help teach us, someone to mentor us or to help us physically or spiritually. It may seem random and coincidental, but it is not. God knows and loves each and every one of us. He wants to help us through his people, as we journey towards Heaven.

CHAPTER 13

"A good player stays focused on the ball... the ball being my Son, Jesus."

By the spring of 2002 my marriage was lost. Although it was sad to end the marriage we continued to remain friends.

When Jesus initially came to me, he started placing people in my life who surrounded me with love. He explained that with the help of these people, I would be able to complete this mission for Him.

One night I went to bed, and found that my right eye would not close. I started to have a vision and it was if I was watching a large screen television with vivid color. The beautiful color was indescribable. The first thing I saw was a bocce game, with the ball standing out in front of me and the players behind the ball. I then saw another vision of sick children. Some wore hats because they had lost their hair. It was clear they were under medical treatment. Others had canes or were in wheelchairs. Then the vision stopped and the Blessed Mother appeared. "My Mother, can you explain this to me, I do not understand?" She explained the vision, "A good player stays focused on the ball... the ball being my Son, Jesus. The children in the street are sick and have no place to go. This is what you will do for me now. You will help these children." "How and when will I meet them?" "You will meet a woman, she is of me; she is of my world," she said. She works with these children; this is how you will connect with them. This is where I want you to work now, with your angel." After the Blessed Mother left I prayed the rosary. As I was going to sleep, Jesus came to me. "You will receive two cards and when you receive them, you will know and have direction." Not long after, I sat with a woman who was studying to become a nun. She told me about a woman she knew who worked with children with cancer, and asked if I would meet with her. Several days later, I spoke to this woman, Midgie, a registered nurse. She had co-founded a local nonprofit for children with cancer, and asked me about one of her very sick children. St.Michael gave her all the necessary information. She was very skeptical, as she had been through this once before with someone who claimed to have a spiritual gift, and afterwards she was disappointed. However the information that Michael gave her transpired exactly as he said it would, and that helped Midgie gain confidence in him. She, her sister and I had lunch, and they gave me their business cards. Later at home, I put the cards on my desk. As I was falling asleep, I heard Jesus say, "You received your two cards today." When I got up the next morning, I went to my mailbox expecting the cards to be there. Just then, Jesus said, "No, the cards are on your desk." I went to my desk and turned the light on and could see Jesus's hand pointing to the two cards. He said, "These are the two women I was speaking of. You will be working with them, to help My children."

Working more and more with Midgie, I noticed that she was somewhat reserved. Because of Midgie's previous negative experience, I had to continually prove that I was speaking to one of God's angels. I did not know at the time that she was a very prayerful person. She would ask God for a sign to prove to her that I was working for Him with one of His angels. She was hesitant and did not want to subject any of the families to anything that was not of God. Midgie had lost her youngest son at an early age to cancer. This is what gave her the strong desire to work with and fight for these children with the same disease.

One night, she was praying again for confirmation that I was of God. The next morning, St.Michael told me to call her. I did, and I mentioned how I kept a journal of everything Heaven had communicated and shown me, as instructed by Fr. Aniello. Midgie asked for some examples in my journal. I told her that from the onset of my training, I kept seeing the number 711. All of a sudden, I heard Midgie scream for her husband. She said, "Maureen, you are not going to believe this, but my son was buried wearing his baseball shirt with his number, 711!" Midgie then knew that this was the sign she had been praying for. She had received her confirmation that I was working for God.

"I was Midgie's best friend when on earth."
Midgie and her husband were about to go to Canada to look into a new treatment for cancer. Although she had received her sign about me, she prayed to Our Father, "If this woman is of You, please give me another sign." While Midgie was in Canada, I felt Michael's presence one night. I then saw a small thin woman. Then I heard him say, "Do not be afraid. This woman has permission from Our Father to speak to you. Do not say anything, My Little Star. Just listen first to what she has to say." The woman seemed shy and stayed back. "You do not know me, but I became Midgie's best friend when I was on earth." she said. Her voice was soft and meek. "I was very sick and Midgie took care of me. We promised each other that whoever died first would return to give the other confirmation of the afterlife." She had tears in her eyes. I explained to her that I did not know Midgie very well and was hesitant about relaying this story to her. I asked for more information. She told me that towards the end of her life, she thanked Midgie for taking such good care of her, and said that no one could ever fill her shoes. She said if I told Midgie this, she would know that I had spoken to her. I asked why she was crying and she said, "These are tears of joy, as you are going to help so many of these sick children. Midgie will also be helped by Michael, as she has many health issues she is unaware of." I assured her that I would do everything possible to get this message to Midgie and follow through to help her. When she left, I asked Michael if I should tell Midgie about this message and he told me I should.

The next morning I called Fr. Aniello and relayed my experience to him and also asked if I should reveal this to Midgie. I wanted to make sure I was discerning properly as well as respecting my spiritual director since I was under his guidance. Jesus had told me many times to be very careful when relaying supernatural communications. Fr. Aniello went to his chapel and prayed about it. He then said that God the Father had permitted this and that I was to tell her what had transpired. When Midgie returned from Canada, I called and told her of my experience. She started crying and confirmed that everything I said was accurate. She was now convinced that I was speaking to Heaven and was sent to help her. Thus my work with the children began.

When I met Midgie at the house, I was surprised to find it very dilapidated, along with a rundown trailer in a field. Midgie and two other people were working inside. They had purchased the old house intending to renovate it so children and their parents could stay at no cost when undergoing cancer treatment at the local hospitals. Midgie showed me the architectural plans for a beautiful building and said that, hopefully, they would have such a building someday. Having been in the building industry, I realized the magnitude of this project. It would be a huge undertaking. Before I left, Midgie introduced me to one of her volunteers named Katie. Katie took one look at me, and excitedly told Midgie, "This is the woman I told you about that came to the hospital a long time ago and gave all the children the toy bunnies!!!" Midgie turned to me in surprise and said, "How did you know?" I replied, "How did I know what?" She then said, "The little bunnies, Maureen, that is our logo!" I smiled and simply said Jesus told me. When I went home, I prayed to Michael and asked about this house. St.Michael informed me that I would be assisting in providing a facility for these sick children undergoing treatment. I would go to the trailer several times a week to help with fundraisers and gradually we got started. Halfway through, the finances were looking very grim compared to the exorbitant costs before us. The four of us would sit in the trailer and ask St.Michael if we would ever have enough money to complete the facility. St.Michael reassured us that the money would come, and gradually, more people came along who contributed. Sometimes it was St.Michael who helped with fundraising, even suggesting who to send letters to.

"Midgie's Heart"
Michael kept repeating over and over again the seriousness of Midgie's health, in spite of her healthy appearance. She was very energetic and happy. He said she had a serious heart condition, with high blood pressure. I knew he alerted me because God wanted her to stay on earth longer to help the children. Therefore, her health issues needed to be addressed. That night, I prayed to the Blessed Mother and asked her about Midgie's health. She told me that Heaven wanted this woman's beauty to remain on earth, for she had helped so many of their children. She continued to say that Midgie was a light that had guided many. The next day, I met with Midgie and told her of Michael's concerns. Now a firm believer in the angel, she listened and went to the doctor, where she

learned she did have high blood pressure. St.Michael then advised her to see a heart specialist. She saw several cardiologists and not one could find anything wrong. Midgie was confused now, because she believed St.Michael, but the specialists could not find a problem. I prayed to St.Michael again for more detailed information. He said Midgie needed to go to a particular hospital and the problem would be found. Not long after she started getting chest pains and made an appointment with the cardiologist the angel suggested. After a few tests, this doctor confirmed that she did have a serious heart condition. Thankfully she was treated with medicine and the doctor continued to monitor her heart.

"The Beautiful Lady Holding a Baby"
In the meantime construction of the new facility was underway. St.Michael even suggested we add a game room and a comfort suite or end of life suite. This suite would be where the child and family would live during the end stages of cancer. The plasterers were working on the walls one day when something very special happened while I was away. A beautiful lady holding a baby appeared to two of the plasterers. They were completely amazed and said there was absolutely no way this woman could have entered the house without ringing the door bell with someone letting her in. They said she just appeared before their eyes, and she vanished. They searched the house, and found no one. One worker went outside to look for her and out front, he found a shiny medal in the mud. He picked it up and ran to the office, and excitedly told Midgie and the secretary about the woman who appeared

with the baby. Showing them the medal, he asked if they knew who dropped it. It was a perfectly clean Miraculous Medal. The next day I called for St.Michael and asked if he knew anything about this. He said I should pray to the Blessed Mother and ask if she appeared to the workers the previous day. That night when I prayed, she confirmed that it was her. I asked why she had appeared there in my absence. She said that it would be more believable if I were not in the building as many people knew of my gift. She appeared in order to increase the faith of those that were working there.

Throughout the building process, I would ask the Blessed Mother if I was going in the right direction because of the long struggle to get the building completed. She continually confirmed that this project was 'of her and her Son' and that she would always be there to watch over her ill children.

When the house was finished, we worked on making sure all the programs were in place, so the facility would run properly. We added a manager's apartment where I lived for a year, until the house was running smoothly. During that year, as families were coming and going, St.Michael guided Midgie and me step by step to implement the programs. St.Michael and I worked with this organization for the next eight years and I witnessed countless miracles. The children's optimism and enthusiasm, despite their illnesses, greatly inspired me. St.Michael did tremendous work with these children, from simple things like picking out their favorite toy to performing astounding miracles.

The following are just a few of the miracles I experienced with St.Michael during this time:

"The Birthday Gifts"

One week we had a teenage boy and a nine year old girl who shared the same birthday. Midgie sent me out to buy their gifts knowing they would be chosen by St.Michael. While driving to the mall, he described what each child would love. The boy wanted a blue diver's watch, and the little girl wanted a particular book on elephants. St.Michael was explicit. He directed me to wrap her book in purple paper, her favorite color. Needless to say, both were delighted with the exact gifts they had wished for. The boy's mother was in disbelief. She said, "This is the watch he has been wanting, but I couldn't find it in blue! How did you know?" "An angel picked it out!" Midgie said with a smile and a wink!

"A Small Miracle"

At a cookout for the children, St.Michael brought to my attention a little boy who had pain in his legs. I asked if his legs were bothering him and he tearfully asked how I knew. I smiled, took his hand and led him to an activity where he could sit to relieve his discomfort. His attention shifted to the cookout and he soon forgot about his leg pain. Sometimes the miracle was as small as knowing someone's needs, as was the case with this boy.

"A Typical Day at the Hospital with Midgie"

One day I went to the hospital. Midgie and her sister had concerns about one of the children they suspected was being abused. The little girl would not speak about this nor would the parents. Midgie asked if St.Michael could give us some help regarding this child. St.Michael explained that this child had two fathers, the biological one and a step father. He pointed out which father was abusing the child. He described the man... his rings, clothing and tattoos. Midgie immediately knew which parent he was referencing. With this help from St. Michael, Midgie was able to resolve the problem and end this child's anxiety. Next we went to the children's ward. Midgie went from room to room visiting every child daily. While on the elevator, St.Michael told me that there was a baby in another part of the hospital that he wanted us to visit. We then went to the child's room and found the mother of the baby very distraught due to health and family issues. It was not long before St.Michael guided her through me and this mother found great peace and comfort. This became a rather typical day working with St.Michael, Midgie and the sick children.

"My Son will extend her time (on earth)."

After volunteering there for a while, I found that some of the families staying there had heard about St.Michael. One day I received a call from a family who had a little girl dying of cancer. They asked if I would sit with her. As I approached her room, I saw a stick figure drawing on the wall she had created. It represented Heaven to her. St.Michael told me to tell her that I knew she drew this with great belief and faith. The little girl cried and asked me how I knew that. She said she was taught this in Catechism class..."To believe." He also told me to tell her that she loved to play and watch baseball, when she was younger. St.Michael was showing this little girl that there was an afterlife. A few months later, her aunt called and told me the little girl was in a coma and there would be a family meeting with the doctors to discuss removal of her life support. She asked if I would pray and see if there was any direction regarding the decision. I immediately went into prayer and called for the Blessed Mother. "My Son will extend her time," she said. I called the aunt that night and shared this message. Due to the dire circumstances, the aunt had difficulty comprehending it, but the next morning she called back, saying that in the middle of the night the girl had come out of her coma and was disconnected from life support. The girl sat up and told her parents and aunt, "When I was sleeping (she didn't realize she had been in a coma) Jesus came to me and told me that He would extend my time on earth, so I could see my cousin's baby be born."

This was Heaven's way of showing the family that God exists. The girl lived long enough to see the baby born. She then was readmitted to the hospital in critical condition. The family asked me to sit with her. I called for St.Michael and he said the girl did not want her father to pursue a legal matter because he had a very serious heart condition. The little girl was fearful this would affect her father's heart adversely. Apparently, the father was considering a malpractice suit, because he felt his daughter had been misdiagnosed. I explained this to the father, as his daughter nodded her head. The father then reassured his daughter that he would not pursue any legal action with the doctor. Shortly after this, the little girl died. St.Michael instructed me to give the father two particular prayer cards at the funeral, one of the Blessed Mother with the "Hail Holy Queen" prayer and the other of Jesus with a "Sacred Heart" prayer. The father later told me these prayer cards got him through the painful loss of his beloved daughter. He kept them in his wallet and would read them whenever he was grieving.

"My Piggy Bank"
The children learned that angels care about small things too. No question was too trivial. At birthday parties and other events, I got to know every one of them. While attending a Christmas party one year, Midgie asked me to take a lot of pictures of a particular little girl. She was very ill and Midgie did not expect her to be with us much longer. I went home that night and prayed to the Blessed Mother. I asked if she would intercede to Jesus for the little girl's health issues to be lifted. She was barely seven and I felt it would be so unfair if she died so prematurely. I then pleaded with Jesus to let her stay on earth. I prayed to the Blessed Mother and asked her if Jesus would allow her to stay. "Miracles do happen," I heard her say. I then went back to Jesus and asked him to use some of the coins in my "piggy bank," to leave this little girl on earth. He did not answer, He just performed the miracle! Years later after I had left the charity I was told that the girl was still with us!

"Interference"
Occasionally I would still receive interference from the evil side for doing God's work. I awoke late one morning

and was surprised to see almost two feet of new snow. I was assisting with an event for the children and didn't want to be late. I went outside to clear the snow off my car. I went back inside to get my keys which hung in the kitchen. My keys were missing, with only my husband's car keys hanging there. I then went to the drawer where I kept the spare key and it was missing too! This event was very important and I did not want to miss it, so I ran back outside and shoveled out my husband's car, causing more delay. I was now late for the event which frustrated me even more. When I returned home late that night, I happened to glance at the hook in the kitchen and sure enough, my car keys were hanging right there. I ran to the drawer and my spare key was in plain sight. I asked my husband if he had found them while I was away, and he said no. I realized then that Satan was not happy with me providing Heavenly help and he had no intention of letting up on me.

"Heavenly Tears"

I continued the work with the children as God had asked me to do. One of the rooms in our new facility was a bereavement room for parents who had lost their children. In this room was a beautiful 30 inch high statue of the Blessed Mother. This statue brought much peace and comfort to all, regardless of their faith. I received a call from the facilitator of the bereavement group, asking me if I could come up to the room quickly, as she witnessed the statue of the Blessed Mother weeping tears. When I finally met her in the room I walked over to the statue and saw nothing! No tears were seen nor was there any residue of tears on the statue's face. The facilitator was in disbelief saying to me, "I swear to you, there were tears coming down her face! I don't know what happened; now they're gone." I called for the Blessed Mother and she confirmed that this woman's experience was real. Little did I know this woman was going to be diagnosed with cancer and this manifestation was a gift to strengthen her faith. I then asked the Blessed Mother, "My mother can you put more tears on the statue for me to see?" "My Love, keep your faith,". Her answer made me realize that she performs these types of miracles to increase one's faith and to show she exists. I asked myself, "After all the miracles I had witnessed, did I really have to ask her to repeat this manifestation?" Sometimes, despite witnessing so many miracles in the course of my training, the human side of me still wanted to see these supernatual things! Shortly thereafter, the house manager made us remove this beautiful statue of the Blessed Mother from the house. He and his wife lived on site, overseeing the home. The woman's husband had been aware of my gift for years and would go out of his way to deride and mock me. He had little faith, and took great pleasure in laughing at me in an insulting, contemptuous manner. He did not want Christmas lights on the house, nor would he allow the statue of the Blessed Mother on the premises!

"The Missing False Teeth"
Several years later, the house manager's wife called and begged me to come to their apartment. Apparently her husband's new set of false teeth, were missing. She told me he had taken them out the night before and they had

just vanished into thin air. Both she and her husband had turned the apartment upside down searching for the false teeth, to no avail. She pleaded with me, "Maureen, please come and help us!" I did not want to help them because of all the aggravation they had put me through. I thought, now we will see how he likes it! But then I reflected on my training and knew I had to at least ask St.Michael what to do, because this could be an opportunity to convert this man's heart. Michael said, "We will go there and get his teeth back." I called the woman and told her I would come see what we could do for them. I armed myself with rosary beads and blessed oil. When I arrived, they were sitting with some relatives, talking. One of the women in the group asked what I was doing with the rosary beads and blessed oil. I replied matter of factly, "I am going up to the apartment to get his teeth back!" "Get his teeth back?" she said in a derisive manner. "Yes," I said, "I believe Satan has taken his teeth and I trust that they will be returned to him!" "Oh yeah right, I have to see this!" the unbelieving man said sarcastically, "I looked everywhere and those teeth are nowhere to be found!" I said I would see that his teeth were returned, and asked if anybody was willing to accompany me up to the apartment to pray; only one woman came along. As we were going upstairs, I could sense Satan's presence as I blessed the walls with crosses of the blessed oil. I started to pray, "Please, Jesus let these teeth be returned to me, so I can show this man that you do exist!" I prayed with all my might, but I saw nothing and heard nothing. "Please Jesus, show him Who has the power! This man has been tormenting me for years, please Jesus, show him!" I had my arms extended up, pleading. Suddenly the false teeth manifested in my hands, instantly appearing right in front of my eyes! The miracle had been completed by Jesus! The woman that was praying with me could not believe what she had just witnessed! She started screaming, "I can't believe it! I can't believe Jesus returned his teeth!" We went back to the living room and I walked up to the man and confidently asked, "Are these the teeth you've been looking for?" He was confounded and completely speechless! In complete shock and awe, he answered, "Yes, yes! Where did you find them?" I explained to him, "It was Satan who took your teeth and is is Jesus who returned them to you!" While staring at me with his mouth open, I recalled, "Remember the beautiful statue of the Blessed Mother that you made us remove and the Christmas lights you vetoed? Maybe now, you'll have more faith in God!" I said Jesus and the Blessed Mother do exist, as does Satan. I continued, "It's time now for you to return to Jesus and let go of your bitterness and unbelief!" The room was so quiet. All were at a loss for words. Once again, Jesus performed a miracle for more than one purpose. Only God knows why that particular group was present that day to witness this miracle. We do not know what they might be facing in the future. It may have been to boost their faith, only God knows.

"No task is too small for St. Michael."
Over the years I had many calls from the nonprofit staff, all asking for help with one situation or another. Many were simple things like missing keys, etc. One time a staff member was preparing to take a child for treatment. She

did not want to be late and could not find her car keys. Michael came to the rescue and gave the precise location of the missing keys. One lady lost the non profit's charge card. St.Michael told her that when she returned from shopping and was unloading the items on the counter it had gotten stuck on the bottom of a popcorn box. He even told her which cabinet the box was in. No task was too small for Michael to help with.

At this time, I was living in a condo outside Boston. The complex had a beautiful pool, and I had promised one of the sick children that I would take her swimming. We pulled into the parking lot and I ran inside my condo to get her a beach towel. Rushing, I accidently locked my keys inside. My neighbor happened to be there and offered to get a screwdriver so we could pry the door open. We were about to try when I heard St.Michael say, "I will let you in." I told my neighbor what St.Michael said, as she was a believer. I placed my hand on the doorknob and it opened immediately! "Let this little girl enjoy her day," St.Michael said. My neighbor was speechless.

"The Snow Storm"
One January day I made plans to meet a friend who lived 45 minutes away. Since I had not seen her for some time, we became absorbed in conversation catching up on all the happenings of the past year. A few hours later, I glanced towards the window and saw the headlights on my car flashing! I then noticed the weather had turned to blizzard like conditions and there were at least three inches of snow that had accumulated on my car. I remember saying

to my friend, "Oh great. I don't even have gloves with me."
I gave my friend a quick hug and as I dashed out the door,
I noticed my insulated gloves right there on the counter. I
was in disbelief, knowing I had left these gloves at home.
I suddenly heard St.Michael say, "Quickly, we must get
on the road, so we can get home safely!" St.Michael again,
helped me greatly, first by alerting me with the flashing
headlights and then by manifesting my gloves for the trip
home!

"The Baby in the Stroller"
I remember running an errand one blustery day. As I drove
into town the snow started to fall. I had to park my car at
an angle as there was limited room to back up in this particular lot. When I came out, I started brushing the snow
off my car, and noticed a woman in a minivan pull into
the spot next to me. She slid the side door open, took out a
baby stroller and put her baby in it. A few minutes later I
jumped in my car, and put the car in "reverse", but the car
would not move. I then put the car in "drive", and repeated
this several times but the car would not budge. I got out
to look under the car and behind it, and at the back I discovered the infant still strapped in the stroller wedged under the rear bumper! By this time the mother was panic
stricken. She said she had gone into the van to get her
purse and when she turned back, her baby had vanished!
Apparently the wind blew the baby in the stroller behind
my car! When I got back in my car, I heard St.Michael say,
"I saved a baby today." I put my car in "reverse" and it now
moved easily. I was so grateful to St.Michael for saving
this baby's life and helping me.

"St. Michael gives the children encouragement."
One day, we had an overnight party at a local inn. The next morning two girls who both had leukemia were knocking on my door. They knew about St.Michael and wanted to talk with him. He gently and kindly gave them details about their classmates, etc., information I wouldn't know. For example, one little girl liked a boy with curly red hair. They were so intrigued that they did not want to leave my room. St.Michael told them they were beautiful and loved by God. After the girls left, I talked to St.Michael, and he explained that he came to these girls to show them that God and His angels were always watching over them. "So when they struggle with their illnesses, they will have these memories to hold on to," he said. They would have hope and know there is a Heaven.

There was a girl in remission who was concerned about going to college. I sat with her and Michael gave her encouragement, telling her not to be afraid. He reassured her she would do well and encouraged her to focus on areas she would excel in, such as clothing design and writing. She was absolutely astounded that Michael targeted her favorite interests. St.Michael was urging her to move forward with her life, despite her illness. She listened and applied his advice and is now living a very full life. Whenever I would ask St.Michael about a sick child, he would come immediately, always with the perfect answer. Jesus, the Blessed Mother and Michael had gone to great lengths to help the sick children we worked with. They would clear the path so I could get the information to the correct person in order to help the child.

I reflected on the vision the Blessed Mother had given me prior to this. The children in the street playing bocce ball, with no place to go. I remembered her saying, "A good player always keeps their eye focused on the ball, the ball being my Son, Jesus." Finally the vision had come full circle and the project was completed. I asked the Blessed Mother if I would ever receive these visions again. She explained to me that if they wanted me to change course or take on a new direction, I would have these visions. This is how they would direct me.

CHAPTER 14

Stories of God's Love

Wanting always to obey the Blessed Mother by staying focused on Jesus, I continued to help the children and others in need. Every day, I continued to pray for guidance and protection.

I would like to share a few more of these stories with you. I find them to be valuable teaching tools from which we can all learn something.

"9/11"
It was September 11, 2001 and like the rest of the world, I was in shock to hear of the the attack on the World Trade Center in New York City. That night when I went into prayer I asked the Blessed Mother what Heaven thought of such a terrible act. She said, "Keep my heart inside of you. Harm has come to many. Many have forgotten about me." She was saying that if we all lived our lives according to Heaven's ways, such a horrendous attack would never have been committed.

I began sitting with more and more people after this. People needed to mourn and try to make some sense out of this catastrophe. Most turned to their faith in God for strength and solace. I met a wonderfully generous woman who helped me to meet with larger groups of people. After I had helped her and her daughter, she graciously offered me a suite at the hotel she managed. Here I could sit with large groups with St.Michael assisting with people's various illnesses and problems. Meeting with people at this faster pace, I noticed many asked the same questions over and over again. At times, I would get frustrated and say to St.Michael, "Here we go again, with the same question!" He was quick to set me straight. "If the question is important to that person, it is important to me."

"Heaven cares about both big and small issues."

Sometimes I needed to be reminded how much Heaven cared about all our concerns, both big and small. I had a woman with terminal bone cancer visit me and she only had a short time to live. She had several questions. I called for St.Michael but Jesus answered. "Tell this woman that I have heard her prayers ever since she was a small girl, praying to Me while riding on the school bus." As I shared this with the woman, she burst into tears saying she indeed prayed to Jesus every day on the school bus. She loved to travel and was concerned about traveling with her illness. St.Michael assured her that she was able to safely travel with her condition and encouraged her to do so. This woman who was expected to die within six months, began traveling again and lived another three years.

"God knows who is sitting in front of me"

Another woman came who had lost her son in an horrific car crash. She was pleading with me to ask St.Michael for any information about her son and the afterlife. But St.Michael did not respond to me, nor did the Blessed Mother or Jesus when I reached out to them. I apologized to the woman and explained that from time to time this would happen. She was very upset. I then suggested that it might be in her best interest to join the bereavement group at the charity where I was volunteering. When I was home alone that evening, I called for St.Michael and asked why there was no response for this woman. He told me she was looking for any confirmation of the afterlife because she planned to take her own life so she could be with her son. I was later told that the woman had joined the bereavement group and was coping much better. I now learned why we should never seek out fortune tellers. This case was a good example, great harm could have come to this woman if she had been given the confirmation she was looking for.

"Our Father wants His children to be loved."
Another woman came to me about her son. She was very disturbed and said "I'm worried that my son has sinned and is going to Hell because of his homosexual lifestyle." I had no idea how to respond, so I called for St. Michael. Instead, the Blessed Mother answered. "A sin is a blemish, an imperfection within the individual." She then instructed me to tell the woman this: "God made all His children differently and He loves each of them for who and what they are. More important than sin, Our Father wants His children to be loved. (by their parents) She went on to say that when it was time for the woman's son to go to his eternal home, it would be Our Father who would judge this.(As with all of us.) We should not judge. The woman looked up through her

tears and said, "I am not worthy of this. I cannot believe the Blessed Mother came to speak to me! I've sinned and done so many wrong things. Why would she come and speak to someone like me?" The Blessed Mother responded, "When I was on earth, Mary Magdalene was my best friend."

"The Piano"

I often spoke with parents of children with Down syndrome, disabilities, or speech impediments. Michael would guide them on the best path, always individualized for each specific child. One mother of a boy with autism told me how her son had little interest in life and was acting out in an aggressive way. "What can I do?" she asked in desperation. St.Michael told me to ask her, "Have you ever thought of introducing him to the piano? You will find if you do so, he will take great interest in this." Two weeks after, the mother called me with good news. Her neighbor was moving and gave her a piano, and her son started playing it just by hearing a song on the radio! He turned out to be a tremendously musically gifted young man and it gave him and his family great joy.

As you can imagine I came to love the children I spent so much time with. I felt so much empathy for them and their families as they were enduring their health struggles. Jesus, Mary and St. Michael always stressed how important love and service are to one another. As our hearts mature in love, our empathy increases, and with that can come pain. I became so close to these families during the worst times of their lives, and they were becoming a part of me. It meant that I was attending more and more funerals, and at times it was unbearable to see the grief these parents endured.

"Hawk, Come!"

A Native American couple we worked with lost their young son to cancer. After the funeral we went to the cemetery. It was a terrible day with torrential rains. A tent had been erected over the grave and all the people from the funeral were gathered there. After the graveside prayers had concluded the father of the little boy, started yelling "Hawk come! Hawk come! Hawk come!" Startled and not understanding this, I called for St.Michael and asked him what was happening. I heard him say, "Wait and watch." The father then stepped outside the tent looking up in the pelting rain and knelt in the mud all the while yelling "God send hawk! God send hawk!" It was heartbreaking to watch this grieving man. We all turned and stared at the sky and at that moment we all saw a hawk circling above the tent. As soon as the first hawk appeared two more joined in and circled above. The father stood up and continued staring at them. As quickly as they had appeared, they disappeared. The father then bowed his head, knelt down and seemed at peace. I later learned that this man believed God sends a hawk to take a soul to Heaven! We have such a kind, loving merciful God. He sent the hawks to comfort this family in their grief! I saw clearly how merciful God was in our times of great distress.

"Ordinary Days at the Shrine"

Now and then I would meet people at the Shrine. One day while walking through the beautiful grounds, I guided a group to the statue of the Blessed Mother. The Blessed Mother told me one of the people in the group would receive a miracle that day. Many of the parents there had lost children to cancer. I relayed her message to the group. As we were praying, one of the women started to cry. She lost a son at a very young age. The Blessed Mother showed this woman her son running and playing hide and seek behind her statue. When this child was on earth, hide and seek was his favorite game. Another mother stepped forward and asked if the Blessed Mother would show her a sign too. I asked the Blessed Mother and she said, "You are her sign." After the miracle was explained to them, they were assured of the afterlife and that God was always with them and their loved ones. They also came to realize that there is a Heaven and the Blessed Mother is most merciful and cares very much about her children.

Another morning at the Shrine people came to me, one at a time, with questions for St.Michael. He gave each and every one of them the information that was most relevant... whether it was emotional, spiritual or physical, anything that would bring peace, joy, love or encouragement to that individual. Some would have health questions, and they would get guidance on an emotional issue. Whatever St.Michael felt was most important, that is what the person would receive. Usually there was complete astonishment in hearing the accurate guidance from an angel of God. For example, one woman had a lump on her breast and St.Michael told her it was benign. He said he was more concerned with what had happened to her as a child. Apparently this woman had been on antidepressants her entire life after her brother committed suicide, believing she was entirely to blame for his death. The woman was completely taken aback that St.Michael knew the details, the timeline and pointed out that she was not responsible for her brother's suicide. He showed her that her brother had a chemical imbalance in his brain, which triggered the depression. St.Michael lifted a heavy weight of guilt from her so she could continue her life in peace.

"What should I do with these religious articles?"
People often felt the need to give me something when I helped them. Of course I wouldn't accept money. I would suggest they could make a donation to a charity of their choice. I received many rosaries, prayer cards, statues, pictures of Jesus and Our Lady. I had so many of these articles and did not know what to do with them all. I asked St.Michael, "My Little Star, we will recycle these religious articles," he said. "Whenever you go out to sit with a group, I will instruct you as to which items you should take and who to give them to." It was truly unbelievable what I started to witness in simply giving away these religious things! For example, St.Michael told me to give one woman a pair of rosary beads from Lourdes. When I did, the woman burst into tears and said, "How did you know? I just returned from Lourdes and lost my rosary beads on the plane!" I gave a prayer card to a man and he exclaimed, "How did you know that St. Joseph was my favorite saint"? St.Michael chose the perfect articles for the people I would be sitting with that day. The pace picked up and I found myself inundated. I was sitting with more and more people.

"St.Michael's Little Gifts to Me"
One time I found myself at home with a high fever and flu like symptoms. I noticed I had no bottled water and I was too sick to go out. I called for St.Michael and told him it would be very nice if I could have some fresh water to drink. "My Little Star, open the refrigerator and you will find the water I put there for you." I went to the refrigerator, opened the door and there on the top shelf was a bottle of spring water. "There, My Little Star, I have taken care of you!" St.Michael sweetly said.

St.Michael manifested something for me on another occasion. It was my birthday and I had poison ivy on my ankles. I tried several types of poison ivy ointments and lotions and nothing seemed to relieve it. I asked St.Michael which medication to buy. He told me cortizone cream would help. I was running so late for my party so I didn't take the time to get the cortizone cream on my way. Unfortunately I had to leave the party early because the rash was so uncomfortable and itchy. When I got home, there on my sink was a brand new tube of cortizone cream! St.Michael then said, "Happy Birthday My Little Star, this is for you!" I started using the cream and within a few days the poison ivy cleared up.

Several days later, I received a distressing call from my mother. She had just been diagnosed with breast cancer. That night, I was praying to the Blessed Mother and Jesus to please allow my mother to live. The Blessed Mother reassured me that my mother would remain here. As grim as my mother's prognosis seemed, I knew that I could count on the Blessed Mother's words. My mother was given 20 more years with us.

"When Jesus performs a miracle, it is usually to serve more than one purpose."

I was noticing that often when St.Michael alerted a person to a health issue, the condition wasn't detected immediately. Other times, a person would have concern for one health issue and get an answer for another condition. St.Michael, a messenger from God, is only allowed to impart information God allows. On occasion, the person would say, "I feel good; I don't think I have that," and ignore the message. Months down the road, the individual would develop symptoms. Many times a person would ask and get an answer that was completely unrelated to the question. They would hear whatever God felt was most important for them at that moment of their life. In the beginning, I asked why, and St.Michael simply told me to trust. At healing services, everyone would pray for a healing but only some would get healed. "It's up to Jesus," St.Michael would say. "When Jesus performs a miracle, it is usually to serve more than one purpose. It is so many can benefit."

"Midgie's Mother"

Midgie's mother was a good person and a devout Roman Catholic but she didn't accept my gift. She had helped her daughter through a very bad experience with a fortune teller years before and was very wary. I was unaware that her mother was admonishing her to be cautious and not involve herself with me. Early on Midgie invited me to her mother's house for Thanksgiving dinner. During the evening, her mother very pointedly told me she did not believe I had a God given gift and that it would be best if I left her daughter alone. I tried to explain to her that this was God's work. I asked her to look at the fruits of my labor. I said, "What's coming out of this? Only good is coming from this work. People are being helped, their faith in God is strengthening." She wouldn't hear any of it and wanted no part of me. That night, I prayed to the Blessed Mother and asked her to give this woman a sign. I needed to keep the path clear so we could continue helping the children. A few days later, I received a call from Midgie's mother, saying, "Maureen, you aren't going to believe this! When I went to bed last night I had terrible arthritic pain in my hands as I held the rosary beads to pray. Suddenly all the pain ceased and I heard a woman's voice saying, 'Maureen is a 'messenger', sent by Heaven.' "Now, in awe, she said she would never doubt me again! That night, I thanked the Blessed Mother for her help, as I knew that Midgie's mother could have become a huge obstacle for me and this work. The Blessed Mother responded, "Continue on." Just as she had promised, she had protected me and removed these obstacles in my path. Midgie's mother shared this story continually with many people until her passing eight years later.

"Good Bye Robbie"
One night, I headed over to the charity to wrap Christmas gifts for the families staying there. I went to the office area and there I found Midgie crying with her sister standing over her. We had just lost a 20 year old named Robbie to cancer and Midgie said she couldn't get through

Christmas without him because they had been so attached
to each other. I called for St.Michael. "Reassure her he's
now free," he said. "He is whole and is with us in Heaven."
Midgie felt better hearing this and asked if it was the
brain tumor that had taken him. St.Michael told us he
had died of a heart attack. He continued, "Robbie is with
us in Heaven. Be assured of this. You must continue on
now to help all the other children." He told her how privileged this boy was to be able to go home on Jesus' birthday. Immediately, we were all lifted up by these words
and were then able to continue with the activities for the
other children. Not long after, Midgie learned this little
boy had indeed died of a heart attack, not the brain tumor.
Several days after his death she found one of his favorite
toy cars on her desk. Midgie asked if anyone had put the
car there, but no one had. When I arrived she asked me
about the little metal car. I called for my angel and he said
he had manifested it for her, with God's permission. "This
was a gift to Midgie, from Robbie, to let her know that he
will always be with her." I have found that sometimes a
person's prayer is granted by God after their death.

"How are you transmitting this information?"
A woman doctor who had heard about me called and asked
to meet. I was always careful to point out that I was merely
an instrument for God and was doing His work, and that
the focus had to be on Him. She asked me some medical
questions regarding herself. Once again, St.Michael responded by focusing on her emotional problems involving
her marriage and children. The doctor sat there in total
disbelief! She shook her head, saying, "Maureen, how are

you transmitting this information. It's completely accurate!" I told her not to try to understand it scientifically. There is a Heaven, there is a God and He sends His angels to accomplish His Will. She just shook her head, not comprehending how this was possible. After meeting with me several more times she started to understand.

"Watching the Watch"

Another time, I sat with a medical student for two hours guiding him through his problems with the help of St.Michael. At the end of our session, he said "I don't understand. When Jesus was on earth, he was poor. Why would He choose someone to do this work who wears an expensive watch?" I was surprised this was his only reaction but I told him I was able to buy the watch by working very hard and that it's okay to possess material things, as long as they do not possess us! We have free will and choices and we must remember the focus should be on God first, not things. Instead of focusing on the information given to him, this man was studying the instrument through which he was receiving guidance. I found this to be a common occurence with many.

"The Football Player"

As a special treat for the families we served, we took them to a theme park in Florida. The kids had so much fun and it was wonderful to see them forgetting about their cancer for a few days. I was thinking as I went to bed about how we could obtain raffle and silent auction items for the upcoming fundraiser. We needed to continue raising money for the organization. I petitioned the Blessed Mother to please give me some guidance for the event. I heard nothing, but thanked her as always. A little while later I felt a presence at the foot of my bed. I looked up and saw a man holding a football and his colored jersey had a distinctive number. He came to the side of my bed and said, "You don't know me, but when I was on earth, I was one of football's greatest players!" Thinking it was another attack from Satan, I quickly said, "Flee, leave me alone!" I rolled over and turned my back to him. He came to the other side of the bed and said he was aware that I was clueless about football. Not believing him, I sarcastically said, "Great, if you are who you say you are, then send me some of your signed memorabilia, so we can sell it at our upcoming fundraiser." "Yes," he said "I will send this to you in abundance!" As this man was leaving, he told me his name which I wrote down. In the morning I told the group about my experience and gave his name. My sister said this man was one of the greatest football players in history!

When we got back from Florida, I went to a sports memorabilia store to buy things for the fundraiser. As I stood in line at the checkout, I heard a bang. A signed autographed picture of this same football player fell off the wall onto the floor. I went over picked it up and thought, "Wow I've got to buy this!" Later I researched this football player and found some contact information. I called and told them about our charity for sick children. The representative was impressed and made it possible for us to purchase about a hundred pieces, at less than their usual price. I was excited to see how successful we would be at selling the football memorabilia at the live auction. The night of the auction the bidding kept going higher and higher! That night, we sold thousands of dollars of memorabilia, making the event a complete success. From that night on, we always put these pieces in the auctions and it continued to be a lucrative way to raise money for the charity.

Only God has the power to allow a soul (the football player, in this case), to return to earth if and when He chooses, to help others. We should not call a soul forth or contact mediums to contact our deceased loved ones because we do not want to open the door to Satan. If we ever encounter a deceased person or any type of supernatural message we believe is from a deceased loved one, we should pray for their soul and leave the rest up to God.

"Visors"
That summer, a man who ran a prestigious polo club in a neighboring state was put in our path. I told him about the charity and he gave us a booth right on the polo field. This was an amazing opportunity to raise money so I started wracking my brain as to what we could sell. The first time around I tried to sell signed sports memorabilia, pictures, posters, baseball bats, baseballs, footballs etc. Although I had a good variety, it wasn't as popular with this crowd, and very little sold. Next, I decided to go into a different direction and have a raffle. I had multiple items such as designer sunglasses and handbags, some signed baseballs, CD players and small electronic items. I thought for sure I couldn't miss with this. Once again I sold very few raffle tickets and was disappointed. By the

third week I was at a complete loss for ideas. I decided to call for St. Michael. I asked if he could help me in my quest for the kids. He responded with one word, "visors." I thought it was a great idea and went online to check out cotton visors at a good price, but all were too expensive. The angel then came to me. I shared my challenge and asked if he could give me some direction. He guided me to a specific store that was having a close out sale on multi colored visors! I bought them all on the spot! My angel then advised me where to find someone to apply various designs to them. The visors were an instant success! They sold out and we met our fund raising goal! Again this beautiful agent and messenger of God, St. Michael, came through for the children.

"The Jump Start"

At the end of the summer I received a call from Lisa, whose sister had a malignant brain tumor and only a short time to live. Her sister who was coming from out of state, asked Lisa not to reveal to me that she had no belief in the Virgin Mary. Lisa also asked if a few others could join in, and of course I said yes. The more people Heaven can help, the better. At the meeting, I started to pray and I called for Michael to help Lisa's sister with the brain tumor. The Blessed Mother replied instead. "I have a message for this woman," and pointed to another woman in the room who appeared to be healthy. "I want to thank her for the beautiful work she has done for my children." Apparently, this woman had worked with sick children as well. She then pointed to a man in the group and said, "Please tell him he must let go of his anger. He is a beautiful individual, but his anger is holding him back." I related this to the man and he started to cry and said it was true. I couldn't understand why the Blessed Mother was not speaking to the terminally ill woman. I prayed silently and asked her why and she said that this woman with the brain tumor didn't believe in her, but the woman's sister Lisa, did. I then related this to the woman with the tumor and she said that after seeing the experience of the others in the room, she was now a believer. The Blessed Mother told her that when she died, she would be waiting for her. When the meeting was over, the same woman told me this had helped her immensely and she no longer feared dying. She truly believed that the Blessed Mother would be waiting for her. This experience not only jump started her faith but gave her great peace.

"I believe there is a Heaven now!"

The simple comments from St. Michael and Mary continued to amaze me. Sometimes I would share something so seemingly trivial, but it would have a great impact on the person. It made me realize Heaven knows us individually and what each of us needs and responds to. For example, I was sitting with a group of people and a woman approached me and began asking St. Michael a lot of questions. I answered her as St. Michael was talking to me. I didn't understand why this woman seemed distant and not understanding me. Then St.Michael said, "She has a hearing impairment, and you must speak slower so she can understand what you are saying." I apologized to the woman, explaining that I was unaware of her hearing problem. Her eyes filled with tears as she pulled her hair back to show me her hearing aids. "I believe there is a Heaven now!" she exclaimed. She hadn't heard any of the answers to her questions, but all she needed to increase her faith was a simple acknowledgement of her hearing impairment!

"Freed from Guilt"
Another day I received a call from a local woman whose husband's mother had died. She said he was inconsolable. I immediately went into prayer, calling St.Michael. He informed me that I was going there for the wife, not the husband. He proceeded to tell me that the woman's first husband had committed suicide and she was taking full blame for it. St.Michael said that her former husband had suffered from severe depression, which stemmed from childhood abuse by his mother. This neglect was mostly responsible for his condition. He stressed that she had done nothing to contribute to his suicide. In fact, he knew she was a good wife and tried everything she could to help him. He said she must not shoulder the blame for his death. She must free herself from the burden of guilt so she could live a healthy, happy life. He also said she should have children, which had been her life long dream. St.Michael then spoke to her husband and gave him confirmation that his mother was okay. He spoke of his mother's beautiful garden that she lovingly kept when she was on earth. This was confirmation to the husband that his mother was fine in Heaven. Both were crying, so thankful that God had answered their prayers and sent them help. She nodded tearfully and said every bit of it was true. Shortly after I received a thank you letter in the

mail from them. She said, "God works in mysterious ways. I can't believe He sent you to me, I have suffered for years with guilt over my former husband's suicide. Now after sitting with you and understanding this tragic loss, we have closure. My husband and I are going to adopt a child and move on in complete peace."

"Chip"

A woman named Jane called and asked me to help her son, Chip, who was flying in from another state. We agreed to meet the following day. We all sat down and Chip asked his mother to leave the room, so he could speak to St.Michael (through me)privately. St.Michael then told him of how he had struggled with various antidepressant medications, that he was frustrated with his depression and was not currently taking his medication. He urged him to follow the doctor's plan for the correct dosage. St.Michael went on to illuminate many events of his childhood, so he would believe it was St.Michael he was speaking to. Chip was convinced and later told his mother that the angel spoke of things that even she wasn't aware of. He was very happy with the meeting, as it had cleared up many of his questions. His mother was relieved and confided to me how pleased she was with the progress he had made since our meeting. I did not realize St.Michael was laying the groundwork for the future of this young man.

Months later, I received a call from Chip, who was obviously off his medication. He and his wife had problems regarding this issue and were separated. He blurted out, "I'm in the woods with a gun, black plastic bags and I'm going to kill my wife and children. I've thought about this and I have it all planned out." He hesitated and then said that something prompted him to stop and call me and try to speak with St.Michael. I immediately called for St.Michael, as I knew seconds were critical because this man was prepared to kill his family at that very moment. I knew I had no time to call the police and no time to call his mother or his wife to warn them. I was afraid if I hung up to do this, he would proceed with his plan. St.Michael spoke to him immediately. "If you follow through with this, you will sit in a prison cell the rest of your life. You are despondent and depressed because you are not on your medication. You don't want to end up in prison. What kind of life is that for you?" Chip broke down and started to cry. St.Michael's wisdom and guidance quickly disarmed him. St.Michael then told me that he was walking back to his car to go home. I remained on the phone with him and could hear him start his car and begin driving. He reassured me that he was calm and that he was heading to his apartment. Once I felt comfortable with this, I hung up and called the others, one being his mother. She later reassured me that she and his wife, immediately got him the proper medical attention, where he was monitored and watched closely.

"Jackie and the Housing Lottery"
I received a call from Jackie, the daughter of a close friend of mine. She wanted to ask St.Michael what was wrong with her. She hadn't been feeling well for some time. I called for St.Michael. He instructed me to hang up with her so he could speak to me first. As soon as I hung up,

St.Michael told me she had a bleed in her head and needed immediate medical attention. I called her mother and explained what St.Michael said. She left work and took her daughter to the emergency room. Hours later, her mother called to say that sure enough, they found a bleed in her head. They admitted her into intensive care, where she remained for two weeks. The doctors told her that if she hadn't come in that day, she would not have survived.

When she was released from the hospital, she and her husband started to look for housing. She knew I had been involved in real estate and thought I might find something reasonable for them, but it was difficult for me to find anything in their price range. This frustrated me. One morning while making coffee, I saw a vision of a newspaper through my right eye. The vision repeated itself several times. I did not understand the meaning of it and went about my day. As I was backing out of my garage, I saw in my rear view mirror an orange plastic bag in the driveway. I got out of the car and picked up the bag which contained a trial copy of a newspaper. I knew there had to be some message in this paper, because of the vision shown to me. When I returned home that day, I hastily ran in so I could go through the newspaper. Nothing jumped out at me. Frustrated, I called for St.Michael and asked why I had seen this vision. "My Little Star, look on the floor." I looked on the floor and there was a flyer that had fallen out of the newspaper. The flyer was about a local housing lottery that middle income people could qualify for. I asked St.Michael what this was about, and he said it was for Jackie. I called Jackie right away and shared this information. She took my advice and filled out an application for the housing lottery. When she arrived for the drawing, she discovered that the lower lottery numbers had the best chance of winning a unit at an affordable price. The lottery numbers were numbered one through one hundred; the number she drew was in the nineties. She wondered why St.Michael suggested she apply as her chances of getting a unit were highly unlikely. Sure enough, she was at the end of the list. In frustration, she came to my house to ask St.Michael why he had suggested this. He told me, "This will eventually look bright for them; tell them to keep the faith and hold on to their number." A year and a half later, I received a call from Jackie. "Maureen, you aren't going to believe this, but we got a letter in the mail stating that we got one of the lottery units!" Apparently, there were many lower numbers before her, but for some reason they did not qualify. The people made too much or too little money, or their credit wasn't good. Because of these regulations, many were eliminated, and so she became one of the fortunate ones. I still did not understand the purpose of this, for many people I have sat with have never received this type of help. I asked St.Michael why Heaven allowed this. "You will see My Little Star. As we go on, it will unfold." Jackie discovered years later that her doctor was going to test her for MS. She wasn't feeling well and asked if I would sit with her. She asked St.Michael if she really had MS, and St.Michael confirmed it and also told her she had other diseases. As time went on, she would be diagnosed with MS, and other auto immune diseases, all at a young age. She struggled to cope with the symptoms and medications, while trying to stay warm and mobile. The unit she received through the lottery was a blessing, as the master bedroom was on the first floor. One night, I prayed to the Blessed Mother. She gave Jackie a message that she would always guide, protect and keep her path clear. As the years went on, I could clearly see how the Blessed Mother kept her promises to Jackie.

"God's Loving Providence"
One day, Midgie and I stopped for coffee on our way to work. At our first stop there was a problem with the drive-thru so we went to the next coffee shop down the street. The second drive-thru had a long line so we parked and went inside. As we entered, we bumped into one of the mothers Midgie knew who had a child with cancer. I had never met her, so Midgie introduced us. Knowing that she was very spiritual, Midgie decided to tell this woman about Michael while we sat together having coffee. I later realized that Heaven had orchestrated all these delays so we would meet this woman. She later told me that the only reason she was there was because her coffee maker had mysteriously malfunctioned that morning. God's loving providence! St.Michael came immediately when I called, telling her through me that she had two sons struggling in school and a daughter who had leukemia. He acknowledged that she, too, had struggles being a single parent. He gave her encouragement and also advice on how to help her sons better their grades in school. Several days later, this woman called and asked if I would come and sit with her and the children.

Midgie and I went to her home the next day. St.Michael began by helping one of the sons who was distraught after the death of his best friend. He gave this boy words of confirmation that his friend was okay. This helped him to be more accepting of his friend's death. He spoke to the other son, who was struggling in school. He explained to him about his learning disability, showing him the origin of his problem, so it would be easier for him to correct. This would help him better his grades and himself. He then went on to speak to the young girl, who was angry about being so sick. She had a violent temper and would kick doors and hit her mother. St.Michael showed her the cause of her anger. This helped her handle and manage it much better. After this meeting, I met with this girl several times. One day, accompanied by St.Michael, I took her shopping and bought her some clothes. St.Michael and I built a strong friendship with her. I heard from her mother often, telling me how much better her daughter was doing.

After a while, however, she reverted back to her temper tantrums. One night, she slipped out of her bedroom window and was missing for several days. Her mother was inconsolable. She contacted the authorities, but no one could find her. Out of desperation, she called me and asked for St.Michael's assistance. First, he reassured the mother that she was safe. He then disclosed that she was staying with a particular girlfriend. Relieved, the mother immediately went to the described location and picked up her daughter. After she came home, there was an incident resulting in the girl being locked up in juvenile detention. Through St.Michael's guidance the mother had developed a strong belief in God. She called me and asked if Midgie and I would come and speak to her daughter's social worker. Prior to meeting with the social worker, I felt it was prudent to meet with the girl herself. We then met with the social worker who asked us why this girl should be released. St.Michael told me to point out all of her good attributes. Several days later, the social worker had a board meeting. The mother and her attorney attended. Her mother started speaking of Michael, my gift and Heaven. Her attorney immediately pulled her out of the meeting and told her this was not a good idea to speak of this, as it may have a negative impact on her daughter's future. The mother stubbornly said, "I don't care. I will call Maureen and they will see for themselves!" Her attorney was adamant that he would be the only one speaking at this meeting. It resulted in him losing the case, and the girl staying in detention. Shortly thereafter, I went back to speak on her behalf with Michael guiding me. This time we were successful and the girl was finally released. Afterwards, St.Michael spoke to her again about how dangerous her anger was and taught her the best ways to cope with it. She took his words to heart, applied it to her life and learned greatly from this. Today she's happily married with two children!

"The Sign"

One day I received a call from Barbara, whose young son was hospitalized with cancer. His vital signs were not good. She asked to meet me at the hospital. By the time I got there with Midgie, the boy had just been pronounced dead. Barbara was crying inconsolably. She had recently lost her mother and was still grieving that loss. Michael proceeded to tell her that she would receive a sign from her mother to show that she was with her and that her son was okay. I wanted to console Barbara so I asked St.Michael if he had any other messages. "No, My Little Star, this is all she will need." I relayed this to Barbara, and she said she would wait for the sign. A week after the funeral, I ran into Barbara, and she had a look of joyfulness on her face. She blurted out, "St.Michael was right! I received my sign from my mother!" Barbara had returned to the cemetery to place flowers on her mother and her son's graves, and that was where she received her sign. She did not go into detail, but insisted it was all she needed. She definitely now believed in an afterlife. This pulled her out of her depression and she was able to return to work. I continue to marvel at how St.Michael works. He is fully aware that some of us need a lot of information and proof before we understand and believe, while others just need a small sign to jumpstart their faith.

"She is not hearing me."
I received a call from a woman who lived near Boston. She had a group that wanted to sit with me, one on one. It was a hot, humid, New England day when I arrived. When I walked in, I saw only two people. She told me that everyone was waiting in the backyard. As I went to the back, I noticed there was no umbrella or cover to shield any of us from the scorching sun. Because of the extreme heat, I tried to keep everything moving along as quickly as I could. I usually had a few team members with me to help with the group, get drinks, help with seating, etc. On this particular day, I asked the hostess to please get me water and a bit to eat. I hadn't eaten all day and was starting to

feel weak and dizzy. As I waited, I noticed the backyard starting to spin and thought I was going to faint. Another woman ran to the hose to get me some water. This perked me up. I found the woman who had been waiting to talk with me, shouting, "I've been waiting four months to sit with you!" "I need my questions answered now!" I said I would do my best to help her but she was really angry, saying, "You better get the information now!" I called for St.Michael, but instead the Blessed Mother spoke. I repeated the information which was not related to her question, back to the woman. Many times heavenly guidance will touch upon something else much more important in our life. Then, I heard the Blessed Mother say, "She is not hearing me." I repeated this to the woman and she said, "You're right! I'm not hearing the Blessed Mother, I'm hearing you!" During my training, I was taught that I would encounter people like this. They were not looking for what Heaven wanted to share with them, they were looking for instant answers to their specific questions. They would not accept what it was that Heaven knew they needed to hear. They would also be oblivious to the fact that I was sharing my time and compassion for the purpose of bringing their souls closer to God.

"Forgiveness is Key"
Another time I had a call from a woman who was hospitalized with leukemia. She had been working in the school system for years. When I arrived at her hospital room, St.Michael showed me her bitterness and anger in a vision of her yelling and berating people. I then saw her in a red car driving very fast and impatiently leaving a

parking lot. I explained to her what I saw and what the angel said. I told her that she had to forgive all those who had brought her harm. She had to let go of this anger because it was hindering her spiritual growth and holding her back. The woman began crying. "You're absolutely right. All my life I've had a bad temper, a lot of anger. I'm responsible for many people getting wrongfully fired in the school system." "This is not our way," St.Michael told her. "Our way is love, peace, joy, with forgiveness and kindness to all. Jesus' way is not for one to overpower another." This same woman was thinking about having a stem cell transplant and wanted me to ask St.Michael if she would make it through this treatment. I didn't expect St.Michael to answer this question, as he rarely would foretell. St.Michael said her body was weak and it would be difficult to withstand such a treatment. He advised her to wait until she regained more strength. The woman was very grateful. "I do know one thing," she said, "I will let go of my anger, forgive the people who have harmed me and ask for forgiveness from those I have hurt. I will discuss the treatment with my husband." Several weeks later, I received a call from one of her children who explained that her mother had proceeded with the treatment. It was too intense for her and consequently it had taken her life. Despite this, her children thanked me for taking the time to help their mother. I believe God sent me to this woman so she could release all her anger before she died. It gave her a chance to forgive others and to ask forgiveness of them. Sometimes the spiritual and emotional healing are more important for our souls than the physical healing. Forgiving is difficult for many of us but if we continue to be bitter and angry the lack of forgiveness hurts us. We can overcome this by asking for God's help.

I had a woman who came to me on another forgiveness issue. Her husband had been having an affair for years and eventually divorced her. She was devastated and very angry. Being a Christian she knew she had to forgive, but of course she soon found it was a lot easier said than done. As hard as she tried she kept reliving the betrayal. She asked me what she could do. I prayed to St. Michael and he said the following, "He (her former husband) has been exonerated. You now need to pray for love." What the angel was telling her is that he had already been forgiven by God. Now it was her turn to pray to God for help, to restore the love in her heart so she could truly forgive as well.

I remember a certain woman, whom St. Michael had told to forgive her husband. After she died, she came back to me through St. Michael with a message. She said, "I wish I had listened to St. Michael when I was on earth and forgiven my husband as things would be a lot better for me here."

"The Three Dollar Prescription"
One sub zero day I was picking up my prescription at the pharmacy, and overheard the woman ahead of me say she did not have the three dollars to pay for her prescription. The woman explained that she lived in a homeless shelter where often her medicine would be stolen. But the clerk was firm: no money, no medicine. I spoke up and offered

to pay for it. The woman thanked me and was given her medicine. As I was leaving, I saw the woman waiting for me out front to thank me again. I looked in my wallet and only had a five dollar bill, and gave it to her. She asked if I believed in God. Of course I said yes, and then she shared that she was so grateful for the five dollars as she had no bus fare for the ride home. She only had enough to get to the pharmacy, and had prayed to the Blessed Mother on the way for help. "I have no money, please somehow let me be able to get my medicine and get home." The woman then exclaimed, "And she sent you!" I told her, "The Blessed Mother is my best friend." She looked at me with tears in her eyes and I marveled at her faith. Many times God will put someone in our path. This can be for a variety of reasons. In this case, it was a person in need of help. We all experience prompts. It could be the Holy Spirit or our guardian angel. It is important to "hear" or "feel" these prompts and then act on them. We may never have that opportunity again to do something for a greater good.

"Linda and Pam"

I received a call from a woman named Linda, who was worried about her friend Pam. She explained that Pam was in the end stages of breast cancer and really did not have any faith. Linda was hoping I would tell her about God's love for her, and that Heaven and Hell were real. When I arrived, I found Pam sitting up in a wheelchair. She was completely disinterested in talking to me. Immediately, St. Michael started speaking about this woman's mother and how she had suffered from schizophrenia. Pam listened but did not respond, St. Michael continued about her mother and then talked about her childhood. Ten minutes into my conversation with her, Pam suddenly said, "Now you have my attention. Everything this angel has said is true!" St. Michael reassured this woman that there was an afterlife and Heaven. Pam then apologized and said she hoped she did not ruin her chances with God. "When Linda told me you were coming over, I assumed you were another fraud. There is no way you would know these things about me. You must be communicating with Heaven!" St. Michael told her how much Jesus loved her and how important it was to acknowledge Our Father, Jesus, and Our Mother. Each time I saw her before she died, St. Michael said things that strengthened her faith and lifted her up emotionally.

I was unaware she had died until St. Michael came to me the night of her death and said, "I have a message for you from Pam. She wants to warn you. Her words to you are, 'bulls and horns, bulls and horns'. Be careful My Little Star." I hadn't a clue as to what Pam was speaking of. The next day Linda called and I related what St. Michael had come to tell me the night before. Then Linda told me Pam had passed. She mentioned that money had been stolen from a family member's pocketbook. She said the family planned to ask me about this at the funeral. Pam had come back to warn me, through St. Michael, not to get involved in this family matter. It started to make sense to me. A few days later at the funeral, I was approached by two family members about the theft. They wanted to know if St. Michael would reveal which family member stole the money. I told them, Heaven will not get involved in this type of situation. St. Michael said, "More importantly Pam wants peace for the family."

Not long after Pam's death, she gave St. Michael another message for me. "Tell Maureen, I now know who she is. She was someone sent by Heaven to help me."

"What about Pets?"
One surprise for me in doing this work was Heaven's concern for animals. I visited an elderly woman one day who thought her dog was having seizures. She was concerned because the vet could not find anything wrong. Her dog would walk around in circles and drop his head. Having heard of me, she asked for help. St. Michael said the dog had a problem with the ligament in his left hind leg and when it bothered him, he would walk in circles. She took the dog back to the vet and asked him to check his left hind leg. The vet discovered the problem and the diagnosis was exactly as St. Michael had said. The dog lived four more years after getting the right treatment. St. Michael said that her dog would be waiting for her when she died. He said anything we hold dear will be waiting for us on the other side. This answered so many questions for others who asked about their beloved pets.

My cat of 11 years was very sick, quiet and vomiting. I took her to the vet but different tests and medications didn't help. I was frustrated and prayed to St. Michael to please tell me what was wrong with her. St. Michael did not say what was wrong, but directed me to another vet that had treated her when she was younger. I took her to that vet, who said she was in pain and terminally ill. He suggested she be euthanized. It was extremely hard for me to make this decision, but finally I agreed. I felt numb leaving his office, without my cat, and cried all the way home. I put my cat's collar under the statue of the Blessed Mother in my bedroom. Just then I heard her say to me, "My Love, my heart is with you." I was begging for God to give my cat back to me. I tried to bargain with Him and promised I would never ask Him for this same favor again. I knew He could do this in the blink of an eye if He chose to. Jesus then spoke to me, reassuring me that when I go to my real home, Heaven, my cat would be waiting for me. Several nights later, St. Michael confirmed Jesus' words. Jesus would not perform a miracle to return my cat just because I was His instrument. He performs a miracle when it is His will and usually to serve more than one purpose.

"The Rosary"

One day I received a call from Ed, a terminally ill man, whose time was short and wanted to see me. I asked my angel what I could bring and he said "Bring rosary beads.", which I did. The following week I visited him again and before I left my house, I asked St. Michael if there was anything I should bring. St. Michael then manifested a pamphlet on my desk, the title was "How to Pray the Rosary". I had long come to the conclusion, not to question, just to obey. The first thing I did when I arrived at this man's house was to give him the pamphlet. "How did you know? This is exactly what I have been looking for and have been unable to find it!" I didn't know that this man was a Protestant and was unfamiliar with the rosary. (The rosary is traditionally a Catholic devotion.) Over the next few weeks, he studied the pamphlet. When I visited him again, St. Michael helped him with some issues he had struggled with throughout his life. He stressed the importance of forgiving his father who had neglected him emotionally. Ed was confined to bed and was on IV fluids. After my second visit, he told me that he heard a voice distinctly telling him, "Get up, you can drink and you can eat!" He doubted, but said, "The next thing I knew, I was up, walking around the house and actually drinking liquids!" Over the next three weeks, this man would open his windows, turn on soothing music and walk around his driveway praying the rosary and learning of the Blessed Mother. Before he died, he told everyone including his pastor about his experience and how devoted he was to the Blessed Mother. I could not believe my ears at the Protestant funeral when the pastor shared how this man had taught her something. She then gave great honor to Our Blessed Mother and proceeded to pray the "Hail Mary" prayer! That night St. Michael showed me a vision of a red rose in his hand and said, "My Little Star, this is from Ed. He wants to thank you for all you did for him." This has happened before, where St. Michael comes with a grateful message from a person we had helped while they were dying.

"God hears all our prayers"
I was invited to a prayer group by a nun. Heidi, the woman who led the prayer group for 17 years, did not want me there because she feared I was speaking to Satan. She went so far as to insight some of the prayer group people against me. The nun who had invited me mentioned this, so I

made it a point to contact the priest who was the Spiritual Director for the group, and talked with him several days before the meeting. After this, he reassured Heidi that I was of Jesus. At the prayer meeting Heidi still would not come near me and was still trying to influence the prayer group to stay away from me. In the course of the evening, everyone was allowed to share their testimonies with the group except me because she purposely skipped over me. Everyone wanted to hear what St. Michael had to say but St. Michael told me to stay quiet, so I did. At the end of the evening, I did sit with each person and all received words from St. Michael. They were all so happy when they left. It was finally Heidi's turn. I sat next to her and asked what she was so fearful of and why she would not speak to me. "You have been the leader of this prayer group for 17 years and your belief is strong." I continued, "When someone is given gifts from God, you should look at the fruits of their labor. Do they have a priest behind them? Is the person taking money? What type of work are they doing? Did the message bring you anxiety or did it bring you peace and comfort? Is it in line with Jesus's teachings?" I was trying to teach her how to discern and avoid fear. I told her how many sick children had been helped by St. Michael. She shook her head and would not listen. But, she must have pondered my words because by evenings' end, she started to respond. When I left that night, it appeared she had made great strides with her unbelief and fear. I asked St. Michael why I was so privileged to have all this knowledge and protection and he said, "Anyone of God's children can have guidance and protection. All they have to do is believe, pray and ask, and they will receive it. Your knowledge is a very special gift from Our Father to help and guide others and show them the way. Our Father wants people to be open, so He can help them. Each person can have a personal experience with God. God comes in the way each person can best relate to. Therefore, we take different avenues to reach different individuals. God tries so hard to save each one of his children. God does hear all of His children's prayers and He will answer that prayer, in the way that is best for them."

CHAPTER 15

Fortune Tellers everywhere!

I had been asked to meet with some nuns at a local hospital. One of them told me she was upset about a custodian who had been laid off from work. St. Michael gave her all the information she needed about the situation and she was completely amazed with his accuracy. Several weeks later, I sat with another nun who was a friend of the first nun. I told her about our meeting and how happy her fellow sister had been. This nun went back to the convent and spoke to her fellow sister about the angel and how helpful he was for her, too. The first nun denied she had ever met me! The second nun was her superior and apparently the first nun was afraid to disclose her meeting for fear of being reprimanded. I understood they had to be careful but still I asked St. Michael, "Why are these prayerful people so fearful?" "My Little Star," he said, "it is because they do not know any better and they are fearful of being misled or misguided, and also question if it is truly from Our Father. Continue to speak the truth of your experiences and what you have been taught by us and let Our Father handle the rest." He continued, "Your gift will help many see Our Father, who do not know Him. Then there will be those who will always believe in nothing, no matter how much you show them."

I was given a book about a famous spirit medium, who allegedly had spirit guides who spoke to her. I had scanned the book quickly, and put it back in the drawer. Several years later, a friend of mine wanted to take me to Boston for my birthday. This same spirit medium was scheduled to appear there and she thought it would be fun to go, so she surprised me with tickets to the event. My friend thought she was legitimate and I did not want to hurt her feelings, so I agreed to go. It was beautiful weather and I was looking forward to spending the night in the city. When we arrived, there was a line of people waiting to see her. While waiting outside we saw a man on a bike ride by every few minutes, calling out, "Stay out of there, this woman is a witch." I called for St. Michael and asked him what the difference was between the gifts this woman claimed to have and the gifts I had been given. St. Michael's response to me was, "You and I, are of Our Father." I knew something was wrong but being curious, I thought we might as well go inside and hear what this woman had to say. While we were waiting, everything before me turned black. I thought I had fainted. I called for St. Michael and immediately my vision was restored. The medium came on stage and began explaining her gift and how it worked. After this, she spoke to people individually. I watched her closely and she seemed to be guessing at times. When she said something wrong, she would quickly cover it up or jump to another subject. She would make broad generalizations that could be correct for many situations. When she hit on one of these, she would expound on it, saying it was information from her spirit guide. During intermission, I was in line for the restroom when this spirit medium turned toward me and said, "The woman with the blue blazer and the white shirt!" I turned to her, pointing to myself and said, "Are you speaking to me?" "Yes," she said, "I can not talk to you and I will not talk to you!" "That's fine. I don't need to speak to you," I said. I questioned why she singled me out, because all I had done was quietly listen to her that evening. The people surrounding me were asking me the same question. They asked if I knew her, but I didn't. I called for St. Michael, and he told me to sit in silence and say nothing. The spirit medium went back on stage and plainly stated that some people think they have psychic gifts, and that she was the biggest skeptic of all. She kept saying she didn't want to speak to anyone who felt they had a gift, only those interested in speaking to her "spirit guide." I listened silently, but I was glad when it was all over so I could leave. While we were walking down one of the side streets back to our hotel, I saw a limousine with what appeared to be body guards surrounding the car, waiting for this spirit medium to leave the building. I slowed my pace, hoping to speak to her alone before she got into her limousine. Sure enough she came out, and I called for her. "Do you remember me? I'm the lady you didn't want to speak to. What's the problem? Maybe your spirit guide and you don't like the "Light" and you don't want someone from the "Light" to speak? Or you don't want people to know you are a fraud?" Suddenly, I heard St. Michael saying briskly, "Leave it, leave it and continue on your way!" The human part of me had taken over. I was so angry seeing this person deceiving innocent people and taking their money for her so-called "gifts." It was hard to contain myself, despite the training I'd received. She quickly made her way to the limousine and left. It felt good to call her out, but I needed to learn more self control.

I was disturbed at the ease with which the average person seeks answers from the spiritual realm with no awareness of where the knowledge is actually coming from. People can become so desperate for answers that they search in all the wrong places. If people only realized that all they had to do is pray to God for guidance. He hears all of our prayers. The Blessed Mother and I have talked about this many times. Heaven has so many graces waiting to give away and all we have to do is ask.

When I got back to my hotel room, the wallet I had left on the shelf was missing. I called security and reported it stolen. The head of security came and said if anyone had entered my room, the code would be in my door, but it wasn't. I reported the incident to the police and then went through the hassle of calling my credit card companies to cancel my cards. By then, it was midnight and I was tired and upset. I tried to get some sleep but only tossed and turned. The next morning at the train station, we put our bags on a table and stepped away momentarily to get coffee. When we turned back around, my wallet was on top of my bag! We were both flabbergasted. My friend asked how my wallet suddenly appeared! It was then I realized this was Satan's revenge towards me for confronting one of his instruments the night before. Later I asked St. Michael why Satan was allowed to steal my wallet. "My Little Star, let this be a lesson for you to stay within Heaven's boundaries when doing our work," he said.

The phenomenon of seeing "black" happens to me occasionally. I've learned it is a warning to be careful of impending danger. A good friend of mine was acquainted with a man who claimed to be a priest. I was told he was very gifted and charismatic. I had been wanting a statue of a particular saint and she graciously offered to send me one. She asked this 'priest' to bless it before she mailed it to me. Upon receiving the package, and holding it, I immediately saw "black." (I was not even sure of the contents at the time.) I then opened the box and saw the statue. I asked the Blessed Mother if this 'priest', was indeed gifted. She said, "This boy embellishes." We found out shortly thereafter that this man was a fraud, pretending to be a priest!

I had another incident with a "fortune teller" psychic when I visited Cape Cod with a friend. It was a nice summer day, and I was looking forward to playing miniature golf. My friend was much better than me and finished first. She walked away while I concluded my game. I then looked around for her and noticed that she had moved her car in front of a fortune teller's business across the street. I walked in and found there were several fortune tellers charging a good sum of money for their so-called "services." While waiting for my friend, one of the fortune tellers asked if I would like a reading for $35. I was curious to see how they operated, so I agreed. She took me into a private room and told me that for $35, I could have two questions answered. For $60, I could have a full reading, which was a palm and psychic reading. I played along and agreed to the $35 reading, as I only had one question. I paid and told her I thought I had a gift and was wondering if she could tell me about it and what it was for. She looked into her crystal ball and shook her head, saying 'they' said I didn't have a gift. I told her to ask again. She 'asked' and the answer was negative again. She asked what kind of 'gift' I thought I had. With that, I began talking about all her medical problems... ovary, knee and ankle...and she was completely overwhelmed with my accuracy. When she regained her composure, she went back to her crystal ball and said, "Yes, yes, they are telling me you have a big gift!" She then broke down into tears and pleaded with me, "Please, please, my grandmother is so sick. Could you please tell me what is wrong with her? I will answer any questions you have, for nothing, if you could just tell me what is wrong with my grandmother." "Yes, I will tell you about your grandmother, but we need to talk first," I answered calmly. I pointed out how she was misleading and deceiving unsuspecting people for money and that it was wrong to take advantage of people this way. "How does it feel to be in dire need, begging for an answer so desperately that you will do anything to get that answer? In your case you are frantic to obtain information regarding your grandmother's illness," I said. Desperate people are vulnerable and are willing to pay anything for an answer to their problems. I explained how disturbing to God this was and how it could bring great harm to her own soul when she died. Trying to help her understand this, I said, "When God chooses an instrument to do His work, it sometimes becomes very difficult for that person, as there are so many people falsely claiming to have a gift and profiting from other's misfortune." The woman sat there with her head down. Guided by St. Michael, I then told her in detail about her grandmother's health condition which she carefully wrote down. She thanked me and tried to return the $35 fee. I told her to keep it and to find another type of job using honest skills. A few years later I was on Cape Cod again and was happy to see that this business had closed and was now an ice cream shop.

I went to a real estate seminar and posted in the hotel lobby was a big sign, 'World Renowned Psychic Here, This Weekend!' The line of people waiting to see this psychic went out the door. My curiosity overcame me and I couldn't resist, so I switched lines and waited to see the psychic. After a 45 minute wait, I got close enough to see inside. There wasn't one, but seven psychics sitting with people. I said to myself, "Isn't this sweet!" I called for St. Michael and asked him what was going on. I was told there was one woman in charge, the 'world renowned psychic' who had taught these other women how to read tarot cards. He told me they were on tour and taking money from people regularly through this deception. When I reached the counter, I noticed a menu of services with prices. I explained to the woman that I just needed the basic service and insisted on sitting with the particular woman that St. Michael had pointed out to me. The person at the desk told me that woman had extra supernatural gifts and it would cost more to sit with her. When I sat down with her, she said she would answer two questions. I told her I only had one. "I think I have a gift, and I was wondering if you could tell me about it and what it is for?" She started flipping the tarot cards over and said, "No dear, I don't see any gift here." I said, "Could you please flip those cards over one more time, because I really believe I have a gift." She flipped the cards over once again and shook her head, "No." She then proceeded to switch the conversation to general information that would hold true for most of us. I returned to my question, and she asked, "What type of gift do you think you have?" "I'll start by telling you that the man in the suit working at the front desk is your husband," I replied. She looked stunned and said, "Continue on." I told her what she was doing was wrong, and that she had taught her fellow "psychics" how to deceive people. "You are taking money from people. You are not giving truthful information, nor is your gift from God. The consequences of your actions could be very dire when you die and meet God." She lowered her head and started to cry. "Yes, you are right, you are right," she confessed. I spoke to this woman for an hour explaining how she was hurting herself and others, and tried to encourage her to proceed in a different direction. I told her that because of her greed, she would be tempted to continue on this same path despite the fact that she knew it was wrong. Several months later I picked up a newspaper and saw an advertisement for her group at a different venue. Unfortunately she had continued on with her misleading and deceptive work.

Later that summer I visited Cape Cod again with some friends. We attended a fair where every other booth was offering some sort of fortune telling. There were tarot card readers, palm readers, psychics; you name it, they were all there! I advised my friends not to partake in any of it, as most likely Satan was behind it or it was someone who was self- taught. "If it were truly someone with a God given gift, they wouldn't be charging people money for it," I told them. As we made our way through the carnival, a man with a crystal ball suddenly stood up and started screaming and pointing at me to stay away from his booth. This man most likely was working with Satan and 'knew' I was working for God and therefore a threat to him. I've learned that if someone is working with Satan they'll know who is of the 'light.' If it is a person who thinks they have a gift or is self-taught, merely having picked up a book on meditation, tarot cards, connecting with spirits, they won't know the difference between the light and the dark side.

The next day I read about a small commercial building that was up for auction. I still dabbled in real estate and decided I would bid on it. I went over to do a walk through and it was then I learned that it had been a fortune teller's place of business. When the bidding started, I quickly realized I was bidding against the mother of the woman who had been running the business. The mother was trying to buy back the building so her daughter could continue with her work there. This only gave me more of an incentive to bid higher, keeping the building out of their hands. I ultimately won the auction, got the building, and had sixty days to close. I knew I had grossly overpaid for it, since it needed to be torn down. After the sixty days passed, I forfeited my deposit and let the building go back to the bank knowing it would not return to the original owners. It is now an office and I feel much better when I drive by.

Another time, I received a call from a woman in a nearby town who wanted to sit with me. I met with her that week, and she immediately told me that she, too, had a gift and reported to a Reiki master. I asked her how her gift worked. "My Reiki master has all the power and he is 'The Master' she said. "Many of us are reporting to him." She said her group had a small business where people could come and get information from the Reiki master. "He is the master and has all the power?" I asked. Then, very firmly I said, "Jesus is the Master with all the power." She was insulted and started disagreeing with me. With that, I ended the meeting. Surprisingly, the woman called me a few days later. She said, "I spoke to the Reiki master and he consulted with his 'master', about you and your gift. He told me that he saw a huge angel with his wings wrapped around you in full protection. He said there was no way to penetrate this and that you were with Jesus. He didn't know who you were, but advised me not to interfere with you, as he was being blocked from getting more information." "It is not about protection, or who has more power," I explained. "It is simply about Our Father, Jesus, and His Mother, who should be our main focus, our light!" My relationship with her grew and I began teaching her very gently about Heaven and God's ways. She was receptive and began to see things the correct way. This made me very happy to help bring another soul back to Jesus.

I have found that there are many well intentioned people who believe they are gifted. This is what they do not understand. There are gifts given freely by God to help others and there are self taught or counterfeit gifts from Satan to serve his evil agenda. When God gives a gift, He insures it by giving the person the proper training and discernment. In my case, the guidance was given to me by God and through a holy priest. Once again, a gift freely given by God, is to be freely given to others, never for self or material gain. The only purpose for that gift is to help souls return to God.

CHAPTER 16

"If I'm going to send you (to serve), I will not tell you, it will just unfold."

I asked Jesus what I would be doing next for Him. He told me, "You will see it as you go." Earlier on, Jesus had said, "If I am going to send you (to serve), I will not tell you; it will just unfold." Most of the time, Jesus will not show us the road ahead. Trusting Him and staying close to Him is the best road map.

I soon received a call from a local nun who told me she was working with Fr. Joe Whalen and his healing ministry. She asked if I would be interested in helping his ministry and I told her I would be happy to. I attended a healing service with Fr. Joe Whalen and his team. He was a late vocation LaSalette missionary priest who had a great devotion to the Archangel Raphael. I remember him saying, "Only Jesus is the Divine Physician and Healer." I was impressed with this priest but still thought it prudent to pray about my decision. That night, I asked God the Father if this ministry was of Him. Suddenly the ceiling of my bedroom opened up and I saw a brilliant blue sky, and I heard God the Father's voice saying, "This is of Me." I was not accustomed to hearing Our Father's voice. I felt very humbled and started to apologize for doubting, explaining that with all I'd experienced, I wanted to discern and proceed with caution. Almost instantly the blue sky disappeared. I knew God the Father was guiding me on this and it was the new course I was about to take.

The next morning I called Fr. Joe's office and asked if he would be my spiritual director since my former director had just moved out of state. "Why yes, Maureen, I've been expecting your call!" Father Joe had a way of making everyone feel special. I was ready for this new mission and looked forward to the people I would meet. From 2008 until 2014, I worked with Fr. Whalen, his colleague Fr. John E. Welch, his assistant Mary Ann and his healing ministry.

It was always awe inspiring to see what God would line up for us when we traveled with Fr. Whalen. While we were on the road conducting healing services, people would ask Fr. Whalen about their different problems. They could be any variety of demonic, family, medical, physical, spiritual, or emotional issues. He would pray over each person individually, sometimes several hundred at a time. When they confided their problem to him, he'd often suggest they speak to me. St. Michael would gently illuminate the root cause of their problems so they could work it out with God. Many times this spiritual block had to be addressed before they could receive all the graces God had in store for them.

In January of 2009 Fr. Whalen, had surgery for spinal stenosis. His assistant Mary Ann was very worried the night before his surgery, as he was 86 years old. She had great belief in St. Michael and had witnessed numerous miracles. She asked me to pray and ask if Fr. Joe could undergo this surgery successfully. I called for St. Michael but heard the Blessed Mother, who reassured us that he would recover quickly. She told us not to worry that all would go well. Just as she said, he breezed through his surgery. He even sat up as they wheeled him to the recovery area and blessed the doctors and nurses thanking them! Within a few days, he was walking up and down stairs and the surgeon was amazed at his quick recovery. In no time, he was back out on his road ministry, just as promised by the Blessed Mother.

I accompanied Fr. Joe and his ministry to several healing services in NYC. The night before, I was told by St. Michael what God expected of me. He said I would be dealing with several situations regarding suicide. On our drive to NYC, I mentioned to Fr. Whalen that a woman would be approaching him regarding a suicide attempt in her family. In the process of setting up, I heard Fr. Whalen calling me. I immediately went to him and noticed a distraught elderly woman who was telling Fr. Whalen about her granddaughter, who'd been hospitalized after a suicide attempt. I overheard Fr. Whalen say he'd been expecting her and that he wanted her to speak to me. I called for St. Michael and asked if he had any words for her. He said "She has prayed to our Blessed Mother her entire life and for that she has been granted this privileged grace. Now she knows we hear her prayers. Tell her to tell her grand-daughter this story and she, too, will believe." This woman said her granddaughter had very little faith but reassured me she would share this story. She was so grateful for this timely help and with tears in her eyes she couldn't thank us enough.

Before the Mass, I was in the sacristy with Fr. Whalen and Fr. Welch, preparing their vestments. All of a sudden, I heard Fr. Whalen calling out to me. As I turned I could see he was gasping for air and being attacked by an invisible force. He could barely get the words out, "Pray over me Maureen! I'm being choked and attacked!" Fr. Welch, who was across the room vesting up, turned and also witnessed Fr. Whalen being choked by Satan. I started praying over him and he was released immediately. I then heard Jesus say to me, "He is of me. Tell him I love him."

Throughout this healing service I met several people who were either suicidal or had suicide issues in their family or among friends. St. Michael gave them all the necessary counsel and direction they needed. Many people waited in a long line to sit with me and St. Michael during this healing service. One woman came in and started quizzing me. She asked about my gift, and how I was transmitting the information. She then said that she had a gift too, that enabled her to smell a particular odor on people if they had cancer. I asked her how this all began and then a deep growling noise started coming from her chest area! "Please excuse this, as it is part of my gift and this happens from time to time." she said. "Years back it started with my reading tarot cards. It's amazing that I am able to tell people if they have cancer." I explained to her that this was not a God-given gift. The growling continued and I told Satan to flee in Jesus' Name. I explained to her that she was actually in communication with Satan. She realized this was the truth and asked what she should do. I asked her if she would be willing to go to Confession and she agreed. I escorted her to Fr. Welch and after her confession, he suggested she follow up with a deliverance priest.

Many times while sitting with someone, they would try to hurry me along, saying "If you have this gift, then quickly get to the point and give me the answer!" St. Michael would say, "God is not at our disposal. We are at His."

We were at another healing service at a well known shrine. While there, our host confided to Mary Ann and me. "We have a beautiful statue of the Blessed Mother on one of the side altars that just turned a beautiful powder blue color!" Curious, I went to see for myself. While staring at this statue, I prayed to the Blessed Mother asking if she was causing the statue to change color. She confirmed she was and said the purpose was to increase the faith of a particular group within the parish.

On another trip, I sat with a woman who'd lost her husband eight years prior. She told me how desperate and lonely she was. She felt guilty even thinking about meeting another potential spouse. She asked me how Heaven viewed this. "When your husband died he left you his heart. In Heaven love has no boundaries," St. Michael told her. He reassured her that her husband's heart and love would remain with her. "Your husband would want you to be loved, and when you die, he will still be waiting for you."

One of our favorite venues was a Marian Chapel and House of Prayer in upstate NY. It was a breathtaking location at the top of a small mountain. The chapel and accommodations were on a rural dirt road, surrounded by fields and woods. It was not uncommon to see deer frolicking on the property. We stayed in the lodge style house; it had two separate living quarters. Fr. Joe and Fr. John stayed on the main level while Mary Ann and I stayed on the lower level. In the evening we would gather in the dining room and catch up on the days events, go over the next day's schedule, and then play cards. One muggy July night, we decided to play gin rummy. Both Fr. Joe and Fr. John had retired for the day and were saying their evening prayers. Mary Ann and I each won a hand and it was exciting as now we would play the tie breaking hand. As we started the final hand of cards, Mary Ann and I began quibbling about the rules. With both of us being stubborn, we had reached an impasse. Just then, Fr. John reappeared and said the ceiling fan in his bedroom had turned on high speed by itself. He said he tried the off switch several times but it would not turn off. Fr. John continued, "As I was trying to stop the fan I could hear the toilet flushing several times by itself! I went into the bathroom to investigate and of course there was no one there. I then attempted to brush my teeth and when I picked up the toothbrush; it bent to a 45 degree angle in my hand!" Mary Ann and I were so fixated on each other's interpretation of the game rules, we brushed this off and barely acknowledged him. Exasperated, he gave up and went back to his room. In the morning we apologized and asked Fr. John what he'd been trying to tell us. It was yet another interference to distract and rattle us from our weekend mission. Being familiar with this type of activity, we actually had a chuckle and wouldn't let it ruin our retreat weekend. It's not uncommon for priests and people doing God's work to be targets of Satan. He sees them as a threat and continually tries to harass them. With complete trust in God, he cannot hurt people who are armed with belief and prayer.

These healing services would prove to be very powerful events. Many people were coming closer to God and Satan could not stand that. We needed to prepare ourselves spiritually and mentally for these services and be vigilant for anything that might come our way. As unpredictable as they could be, these services were rich in healings and full of blessings. I felt very blessed to be part of them.

When we returned from upstate NY, I had a call from a frantic woman who wanted to see me as soon as possible. She said her roommate had put a spell on her, and told her that when she entered their apartment, her cat would attack her and she would become very ill. I called for St. Michael. He said, "There is a very simple answer to this. The only harm that can come from this is self inflicted harm...your own fear. Don't feed into this!" St. Michael told this woman to stand up to her roommate and tell her it was all nonsense! "Do not be fearful and do not fall into this trap," St. Michael instructed. He told me that anything such as spells, curses, voodoo dolls, etc., are nothing more than Satan's attempt to intimidate and instill fear, so stay in the light and away from these things. Much of a curse or spell is one's own fear. One needs to pray for protection from Jesus and trust completely in this. So once one puts their trust completely in Jesus the fears will subside. Satan cannot meddle with your life unless you allow him to. The woman called me several days later. She did exactly as St. Michael had instructed and her roommate ended up backing down. When she entered her apartment, the cat was sound asleep on the couch.

One day I was having a problem with my debit card. I went to the bank to speak to someone, and while waiting, I heard St. Michael say, "This woman you will be talking to has very little belief. She is sick and fighting breast cancer." I started to chat with her and mentioned my gift of knowledge. She immediately asked if I could give her any information regarding her problems. St. Michael began with her mother's health issues, high blood pressure and depression. She confirmed this to be true, and then said how sick she felt and how little faith she had. That is when I told her I knew she'd been struggling with breast cancer. She just stared at me, her eyes brimming with tears. I spoke with her for an hour and she was grateful for my help in bolstering her faith in God that day. "Thank you so much Maureen, I now have the strength to fight this disease. I never believed in anything, and now I know that God exists and there is an afterlife! Wait until my mother hears this!" she said. I reminded her I was merely an instrument doing God's work and that she needed to thank Jesus and the Blessed Mother.

The next week I met with an emergency room registered nurse, who had worked in the trauma unit for over 20 years. She wanted to know why her husband wasn't feeling well. St. Michael then told me that he had a heart condition that would be difficult for the cardiologist to detect. Later that week she told me her husband had seen the doctor, who said his toes were turning blue because of the calluses on his feet. I asked St. Michael again and got the same answer about his heart trouble. (St. Michael will always speak of the most important issue, even if the person is asking about something else.) She then made an appointment for him to see a cardiologist. The doctor conducted several routine tests and told him he didn't have a heart problem. The husband, being a non-believer, just dismissed what was told by the angel and subsequently, his wife gave up. Two years later I received a call from the wife. She frantically told me, "I've never forgotten what you told me about my husband's heart. He had a heart attack last night and is in ICU!" I was glad to learn later that her husband survived.

What I love best about my mission is being able to help so many people. I met a pleasant couple at one of our healing services. The wife, full of faith, had brought her husband to sit with me. Being a detective he saw everything as "black and white." With a wink she said, "Good luck!" and so, we started our session. St. Michael began by telling him about his personality. I could tell this got his attention but he was determined to appear unimpressed. "I have a question for that angel. I'm working on a case and there are several suspects. Can you help me with that?" I confidently replied "This is regarding a missing diamond tennis bracelet." "Now you are scaring me!" he said wide eyed. "Can St. Michael give me a description of the perpetrator?" St. Michael described a female with short red hair and blue eyes. The detective confirmed that this fit the description of one of the suspects! St. Michael reassured him if he focused on this particular individual, the case would be solved. Two weeks later, I received a call from the detective. He told me they had made the arrest, and that it was the woman with the red hair and blue eyes! St. Michael's goal was to prove to him that God and angels do exist. That was the first step to increase his faith. I met with him later on and he asked me about the Bible, Jesus, and the Blessed Mother. He got himself a Bible, began attending Mass, and came to our healing services! Shortly after these incidents the detective fell ill and has had ongoing health issues. Only God knows what is ahead for each individual and sets the course and circumstances for that soul to return to Him. St. Michael did not give this information to solve a crime and return the bracelet. He gave this information to strengthen this man's faith!

One day a man I had known through real estate called me. He was very skeptical about my communications with Heaven. He had even gone out of his way to sabotage my building projects. Now he was calling from the hospital with severe abdominal pain, and left a message on my voicemail: "Maureen, I'm in the hospital and the doctors are running tests to pinpoint the problem. Can you ask that angel, what's wrong with me!" I gave it some thought, then got busy and forgot to ask. About a week later my angel came to me, urging me to call this man. Immediately after St. Michael spoke, I *audibly* heard a replay of a conversation this particular man had with a woman I knew. He was threatening to do me harm because I didn't return his call with the angel's answer! He was furious! I heard the words crystal clear, as if I was sitting in the room with them! I couldn't believe my ears. St. Michael allowed me to hear this for my protection, and then told me to tell this man that he needed prayer. On occasion, when I would sit with someone who was angry and wanted to discredit me or Heaven, it would be St. Michael's way of allowing me to actually hear and understand the problem with the "playback" of a conversation. The next morning, I called the man and told him that the angel said he needed prayer. His curt response was, "I do not understand. I've witnessed other people getting information. I ask and I am told I need prayer?" "I am just the messenger. I can only tell you what the angel told me, nothing more," I replied. In this case the angel knew that this person needed prayer in order to evolve spiritually.

There were some women I knew that continually criticized the way I dressed. I have always dressed conservatively, wearing neutral colors avoiding a lot of jewelry and trendy clothes. They would regularly joke about my appearance. I would say nothing, but it started to bother me so I asked the angel about it. He said, "They will have to atone for this."

I also prayed to the Blessed Mother because I was angry and found these continued remarks hurtful. She gently responded, "Say what I said, Say not of what I have, see me for who I am." Later she said gently, "Icicles will melt." I didn't understand. She explained to me that if we come to her in prayer about an anger issue, she will help melt our cold hearts. A good lesson for me. So many times, I would sit with people who'd become very bitter that they'd given something away, such as money or an object. They were unhappy and had regrets. St. Michael's response to this was, "Give, when you can give with a smile." Having ulterior motives for giving, such as to obtain control of a person or becoming bitter after we give, will only hinder us. We will receive little, if any, merit in Heaven. God always looks at one's intentions.

Although I was no longer volunteering at the charity, Midgie and I were still close friends. In March 2009 she called and tearfully told me her dear mother had just been rushed to the hospital. When I got there, I was told her mother Ginnelle had suffered a severe stroke. She could hear and see but had lost her speech. She was very agitated, trying to ask for something, but Midgie couldn't understand her. I went to Ginnelle's bedside, knelt down and called for St. Michael and asked him what she was asking for. St. Michael said, "She wants her rosary beads put around her neck." I turned to Ginnelle and asked if this was true. She nodded her head for 'yes'. Midgie quickly went to her purse, got her rosary beads and gently placed them around her mother's neck. Ginnelle promptly gave us a thumbs up! Several days later she regained her speech.

The doctors told us her time here was short due to the severity of the stroke. She motioned to me to come closer to her bedside, and with a faint shaky voice, she said, "I need to talk to you. I was on the other side. I will be going home now. Please watch over my grandchildren." She then said, "There will not be a need for you to watch over Midgie. She'll be coming with me shortly." I thought she had somehow misunderstood, but she insisted she was certain of this. I called for St. Michael and asked if this was so, but I received no response. I had no idea what was ahead. Ginnelle remained in the hospital for several weeks before she peacefully passed on. Midgie had been extremely close to her mother and was taking her death very hard. We went to the shrine to light a candle for Ginnelle, and while there, Midgie asked me to ask St. Michael if there were any messages from Heaven or from her mother. I called for St. Michael, but the Blessed Mother responded (to Midgie) by saying, "Hold onto her heart, you will be with her shortly." You will be with her shortly? How could this be? I did not expect that! Now I knew something was about to unfold!

CHAPTER 17

"The Turn in the Road..."

As I mentioned earlier, God taught me when my mission or course was about to change, I would sometimes be shown a vision. It was January of 2010, almost a year after Midgie's mother's death. I was sitting at my kitchen table, when I saw a clear vision of a road with a sharp turn. I was unable to see anything else in the room, just the vision. I called for St. Michael and once again the Blessed Mother came and quietly told me, "Hold on to me. I will walk with you." I was puzzled by this vision. The next day, I met with Fr. Welch and described what had been shown to me. I drew on a paper napkin the sharp turn in the road that I had seen, and asked him what it meant. He said, "All we can do is trust God and wait to see what unfolds with this new direction."

Shortly after receiving this vision Midgie stopped by on her way home from the hospital where she had been visiting some of the children. We were catching up, when suddenly I heard Jesus say, "Take care of her, take care of her." Startled, I asked Him silently, "Why Jesus, is she sick?" He did not reply. I asked again, "Why, Jesus is she sick?" Once again, no response. I turned to Midgie asking her if she was feeling okay. She said she felt fine. Of course I told her what I had just heard. She said, "I feel great Maureen. There's nothing wrong with me!" She spent the night, comfortably sleeping in her favorite chair and left for work in the morning.

In mid-January Midgie called me from the hospital where she was being treated for severe abdominal pain. I got there as fast as I could. She hadn't been diagnosed yet and the doctor's planned to continue with more testing the next day. That morning I was approached by a nurse in the hall. She asked, "Are you here to see your friend today?" "Yes," I replied. "You must put this in God's hands now, trust in God," she said compassionately. Immediately I thought Midgie had been diagnosed. I was about to ask her another question but she vanished. I ran to Midgie's room to see if she'd been given a diagnosis but she hadn't. I didn't share my experience of meeting the nurse in the hall, as it would've added to her anxiety, but what the nurse said kept echoing in my head, so I went to the nurse's station in search of her. I was told there was no such nurse there who fit that description. I now believe this was an angel sent by God, to help prepare me for what lay ahead. After many tests, the doctors diagnosed her with stage 4 pancreatic and liver cancer, and gave her three to six months to live. We were all numb with this news. The next thing I remember was leaving the hospital, shocked and stunned. Somehow I found my way to the parking garage. The moment I got into my car, the radio turned on by itself! The song playing was about missing someone who was gone and the first lyric I heard stopped me in my tracks as it literally described my vision and my question to Fr. Welch about why the road turned. Now I understood...my new direction was about to unfold.

After the shock of Midgie's diagnosis, we tried to remain hopeful. Her friends encouraged me to pray to Jesus for her physical healing, sure that Jesus would grant her a miracle because of all her good work with the children and possibly because of my gift. But I knew I was not assured of any special favors. Jesus would say, "Know I am in control; I know what is best." I would then pray to the Blessed Mother and ask if she would ask her Son Jesus for the physical healing of Midgie. She replied, "You will continue on." Her assurance helped me to move from fear to faith. After ten days in the hospital Midgie was released to begin her treatment. She always remained cheerful, loving and hopeful.

Once again, Midgie asked me to take her to the Shrine. While there, we walked over to the statue of the Blessed Mother. Midgie's son was getting married that June and she was worried she might not live long enough to attend his wedding. That is when I heard Our Mother very tenderly tell me, "Reassure her, she will remain on earth to complete everything her heart desires. She has time." This gave Midgie such comfort and hope. Shortly afterward, Midgie started her treatment in Boston. One night she stayed at my house so I could drive her to treatment the next day. In the morning I noticed on top of her bag, a cross made from woven blessed Lenten palms. I asked Midgie, "How did this cross get here? I just saw it upstairs on my dresser!" She said, "I thought you put it there!" I asked St. Michael. He said, "It was I who put the cross on top of her bag. It will comfort her." I turned to Midgie and told her it was the angel. Immediately, tears rolled down her cheeks. "Maureen, what a great gift."

Midgie continued to work with the children throughout the remainder of 2010. Despite her struggles with chemotherapy, she never let it interfere with her love and care for them. It was now January 2011, the second year of Midgie's treatments. She had been able to spend time with her children and see her son married. Shortly after, Midgie was admitted into a Boston hospital for internal bleeding, possibly the result of the radiation therapy. She didn't tolerate a particular treatment well and began hemorrhaging. The doctors had given her two blood transfusions and said there was nothing more they could do. The hospital chaplain had already performed the Anointing of the Sick. I told her I was on the way, and started to cry, praying to God that I would get there in time. Suddenly I heard St. Michael, "There is still time. She will pull through this." I called Midgie immediately and told her what St. Michael said. She was so discouraged, and said tearfully, "It doesn't look good. The doctors can't stop the bleeding." Sure enough by the time I reached the hospital the bleeding had stopped. Slowly she started to feel better, just as the angel said. Two days after this terrible brush with death, Midgie was released. The doctors couldn't believe it. I called Mary Ann and she asked me how long I thought she had. I picked up my calendar and flipped through the months. I could "see" that she was still alive on certain dates until I got to the middle of June 2012, then I could see no further. I told Mary Ann what I saw. Being a firm believer in my gift of knowledge she said, "Ok, we better prepare."

Midgie, desperate for a cure, was tempted to try alternative cancer treatments in the second year of her disease, searching for anything that promised a cure. She contacted a man who had written a book on curing cancer through diet. The first phone call was $500, and unfortunately she spoke to him several times in an attempt to streamline his diet for her. When she shared the diet with her doctors they told her it would only accelerate her weight loss, and insisted she stop it immediately. She then found a woman that had a "magnetic wand" that supposedly cured cancer. She told Midgie to wave this wand over her stomach area and her tumor would disappear. The cost of the wand was $375, with an additional fee for the woman to come demonstrate how to use it!

Midgie's final attempt was with a woman who claimed to have a gift. She told Midgie that she was her own personal savior, and that it was her choice if she wanted to stay on earth or wanted to die! Midgie was so desperate at this point, she was grasping at straws instead of trusting in God. This was very hard to watch because I knew none of it would help. As the woman was talking to Midgie, I asked her, "Who's telling you this?" She answered confidently, "My spirit guide!" I then said, "Oh, so it's Midgie's choice to live or die, not God's?" "Yes, she can tell God she wants to stay and this will be granted to her." I just shook my head and left. She filled Midgie's head with false promises. When a person is terminally ill, they're vulnerable to any promise of a cure. The bottom line is that Our Father manages our next heartbeat and breath. He has the plan and the answer, and our role is to trust and pray. He always does what is best for our soul and in His perfect timing.

In June of 2012, I heard St. Michael's voice. "She needs you now!" I called the hospital and learned Midgie had been given twelve to twenty four hours. Her daughter brought her home to the "end of life" suite in the home that the angel had helped us create years before. Her daughter and I were there talking to her. Midgie was gazing all around the room and suddenly said, "Can you see them?" "See who, Midgie?" I said. She started naming many of the children she'd helped through the years who had died from cancer, obviously seeing them right before her. "They are all here, can't you see them?" None of us could see them. She began to converse with her mother and Timmy, one of her favorite children, along with a few others she had cared for. Then she turned to me and said, "I will always watch over you, Maureen and if God will permit it, I'll communicate with you." The next day I called Fr. Whalen, and he and Mary Ann drove up from Connecticut. The entire family gathered at Midgie's bedside. He then gave her the Sacrament of the Anointing of the Sick, just as he had for her mother three years before, and then led us in praying the rosary. Midgie slipped into her final coma and never regained consciousness, dying several days later.

Logically, I knew the cancer would eventually take Midgie's life. As prepared as I thought I was for her death, I was equally unprepared, emotionally. Losing my best friend, whom I had shared my life and work with for ten years, left a huge void in my life. There is no schedule for grieving, and I had to trust in God to get through it. St. Michael tried to console me saying, "Sad as you are, sad as you can be, know you will always have me." I was so grateful for St. Michael's goodness and all the ways that he has been so loyal to me. I could not ask for a better friend than my sweet angel. I felt his heart ached alongside of mine. I asked Jesus why He did not allow Midgie to stay on earth, why He did not grant her a miracle. I couldn't understand. Jesus reassured me gently, "You must know I am in full control and I know what is best. You have a lot of her in you now. Our Father sees her fruit and knows you will follow. You will know she is with you. She will live on and My Mother will hold you."

Three days after her death, I heard Jesus' voice saying, "She is with you." "I know Jesus, but it's not the same," I replied. As I was saying this, I looked up, only to see Midgie and her mother standing in my bedroom! They both looked young and in full health. I couldn't believe what I was seeing! "Maureen, it's me," said Midgie, "I am okay and will always be with you." I asked if she was in Heaven and she said, "No, but I am in a very good spot. Please pray for me." I reassured her, that I would pray for her every day until I died. I then asked her how long I would live, but she said she couldn't answer that question, that it was not allowed. Midgie's mother was silent, standing beside Midgie, smiling and holding her hand. "Our appearance to you is a privilege granted by God for the purpose of consoling and comforting you," Midgie joyfully said. With that, they left. I just sat on my bed, taking it all in. I was so grateful to God for allowing me this privilege.

Let me be very clear. In no way did I conjure up the soul of Midgie as this is wrong. I was granted this privilege by the special permission of God; only He can permit or allow this. We are never to call souls forth on our own or through a medium.

CHAPTER 18

"Our Father hears all of our prayers."

A month after Midgie's death in 2012, I attended a healing service with Father Whalen. There were many people arriving from surrounding states and the healing services usually lasted until midnight. It was there I met the holy priest who was hosting us, Father Paul Desmarais who did deliverance ministry in his diocese. He introduced me to a counselor who worked with him on various "demonic" cases. She conducted interviews with people and assisted him in discerning whether or not the case was psychological, induced by medication, or demonic. They soon learned of my gift. This priest was initially skeptical of me and justifiably so, as priests, especially, have to be very careful when discerning the gifts of the Holy Spirit. While driving to meet me he told the counselor that he had a specific question and if it was addressed without him asking he would know that I indeed had a gift from God. After they arrived, we sat around the dining table as St. Michael began guiding me. Fr. Paul was very quiet and his counselor assistant took notes. It was then that St. Michael addressed the very question that Fr. Paul had been thinking of. Astounded, the priest revealed he had received the confirmation he needed and was assured that I was speaking to Heaven. From this point forward, we joined forces to fight evil.

A month later we were asked to meet with a woman named Nancy who had given Satan permission to enter her soul. I accompanied Father Paul and several others who came along to pray. The priest started by asking the woman some questions. "Could you tell me what is good about Nancy?" The woman's head dropped and her eyes rolled back in her head. She slowly raised her head and with a contorted demonic face began glaring at us. She gave an obscene gesture toward the priest and began dry heaving. The priest started his deliverance prayers which had her writhing in agony at every word. I called silently for Jesus. Eventually He came after much prayer by Fr. Paul and myself and expelled Satan from her. Often these prayers have to be repeated before the demon or demons leave. It is not an easy task, and one must prepare with much prayer and fasting and especially with full faith in Jesus. Full faith – meaning total belief and complete trust in the love and power of Jesus, regardless of what is put in front of you. I spoke with Nancy frequently by telephone after this. I prayed and encouraged her to be strong and resist temptation, to stay with Jesus and reject Satan and all his false promises. But after a few weeks, she said she could no longer resist him, started communicating with him again, and reverted to her former lifestyle. She made it clear that she did not want another deliverance. Once someone has been delivered, many times Satan will relentlessly pursue that soul. God will give us graces to resist temptation but He will never interfere with our free will. Sometimes people require multiple deliverance sessions (or exorcisms) before the problem is resolved and the person is healed.

I continue to pray for Nancy and have put her in God's hands. Through the years, I have seen this sad occurrence over and over. I continued my work at this time with the counselor who assisted Fr. Paul. She would call me before she met with various people who were having problems and I would go into prayer. St. Michael would give me the background and insight on these individuals to share with her. She then had all the information she needed before she met with them and could discern more easily exactly what was happening with each case. Many times it wasn't a demonic issue, but a problem such as trapped anger, lack of forgiveness, depression, mental illness, medication, etc.. Without St. Michael's help many of these cases would have been very complex to discern and taken a much longer time to resolve.

The counselor I worked with called about a family whose young daughter was experiencing loud knocking on her dresser and bedroom wall during the night. She said the priest had gone twice to bless the house and to pray deliverance prayers. Unfortunately the activity became worse and consequently the family had to move out of the house. She asked if I would pray to St. Michael for any insight. I prayed and St. Michael told me that the wife was very angry and was blaming God for loses she had experienced in her life. He concluded saying if she forgave God, the activity in the house would stop and she would be abundantly blessed. I relayed this to the counselor and she discussed it with the woman. The woman admitted that she'd had several miscarriages and was angry with God. After being counseled by the counselor the woman agreed to forgive God and go to Confession. After she reconciled with God, the activity in the house stopped. This is an example of how God permits Satan to briefly torment a person, knowing that it will prompt that person to turn back to Him.

Another case involved a woman and her dog. Objects were moving around in her house, and she was waking up at 3:00 AM to the howling of her dog. He would turn and run as if something terrifying was chasing him. The dog became so anxious she considered finding him a new home. She tried a psychic/tarot card reader but this only increased the attacks. She finally called a priest and begged him to come bless her home. She told him that the previous owners of the house had a teenage son who had died from a head on collision under the influence of alcohol. She was sure his ghost was haunting her house. The priest invited me to accompany him. While driving there he asked if I would pray to the angel for insight into this situation. The angel told me that the woman was consumed with trapped anger towards her mother and father. He said she had to forgive her parents and let go of this discord within herself. Once we were there she went into denial about this and insisted she had the ghost of this teenage boy in her house. Eventually she admitted that her deceased

alcoholic father had abused her and her mother had ig-
nored it. She had been angry her entire life because of
this. I told her Jesus was permitting this paranormal activity in her home so she would forgive her parents, return
to Jesus and restore her soul. She now understood the root
cause of her problem. The priest counseled her and heard
her Confession, and then proceeded to bless the house and
the dog. She reconciled with her mother, forgave her deceased father and subsequently all the demonic activity in
the house ceased.

Later on in the year, another priest in a neighboring
state invited me to assist him in a deliverance at a school.
Apparently there was an evil entity manifesting itself and
frightening the children in the school bathroom. The night
before, I was shown a vision of the green bathroom wall
where the entity would appear. The priest started by praying and blessing each classroom, as we accompanied him
in prayer. As we approached one classroom, I felt Satan's
presence. I could feel his oppression as the priest began
his deliverance prayers. Satan started mocking the priest,
saying that he and his prayers were a joke. Only I could
hear this. Unfazed the priest persevered in his prayers
and stayed focused. Satan continued to mock and laugh
at us, which I have found to be one of his common methods of attack. I prayed silently as the priest continued
praying aloud. Satan would not leave and he was taking
great pride in tormenting us. I became very frustrated,
and raised my voice loudly commanding that Satan leave
in the Holy Name of Jesus! It was a long, tiring ordeal,
but eventually Jesus cast him out. After this, the priest

continued to bless each room in the school. Our mission for that day was completed.

That evening, I was abruptly awakened by the torments of Satan. It was in the same way he had tried to frighten me in the past. He would violently shake my bed while staring down at me as a dark shadow, with a derisive laugh. I did not understand why Jesus would permit this after all my years of training. Distressed, I called for the Blessed Mother. She came to comfort me and showed me a vision. It was an instant replay of the former day and how I had not followed Heaven's training. I had raised my voice after the Blessed Mother had taught me that this was not Heaven's way. She showed me that I had lost control. "You must under all circumstances, remain calm and in control, in quiet prayer and call for my Son, Jesus," she reminded me. "He will then swiftly and quietly remove the entity. These are humbling steps." "I am so frustrated," I cried out to Our Father, Jesus and Mary. "I fall down, I get up, I fall down, I get up, I fall down, I get up..." It was then I heard Our Father say, "And that is why I am proud of you." (He was proud that I always got back up after making a mistake and continued on. This applies to all of us.)

I have received many calls from people who experience paranormal activity, from flickering lights, banging on walls, articles being moved, to beds shaking. People commonly believe it is the house or a ghost, but that is rarely the case. It's usually something within the individual, such as a lack of forgiveness or anger. God may permit this for a variety of reasons. They may need to forgive, they may need to find Jesus, or to control their anger. He knows each of us intimately and how to get our attention to turn our lives around. Allowing some supernatural phenomena leads some to find Him through a priest or prayer. My advice is to go to Our Father and ask for help, and trust that help will come.

My Spiritual Director, Fr. John E. Welch, continually celebrates Mass for me. St. Michael told me how important this is, especially when doing deliverance work. In a dream he showed me how Satan tries to attack me, but is being diverted because of the protection around me. He then showed me how important Masses and prayers were for our deceased loved ones and all of us. He said, "Our Father hears all of our prayers." This is so important, as many people think that God is ignoring them when their prayers are not answered right away. Through the years I've learned that almost all of the time our prayer is not answered immediately. Sometimes Jesus will say, "I have heard your prayer," which usually means, "Okay, not now, maybe down the road." The majority of the time the person is praying for something that they will not receive because Jesus has a better plan for them, either for this life or for their eternal life. I always remember what I was taught through my training, that we cannot see ahead but God can; therefore it is best to trust!

CHAPTER 19

"We are going to Hell, aren't we my Mother?"

Months passed but I was still grieving the loss of my dear friend, Midgie. My emotional pain was unbearable at this time. One evening I glanced at a picture of Midgie and her mother when they were both healthy. I was thinking about all the wonderful work she'd done with the sick children when all of a sudden I heard a familiar voice. I knew immediately that it was Midgie's mother. "Maureen," she said, "Midgie and I just came from Mass. The souls here can attend Mass. I am so proud of my daughter, because she is overseeing the cancer centers (on earth.)" "How does she do that?" I asked, thrilled to be speaking to her. "Through prayer," she answered. To know that her mother was happy was such a relief. It eased my sadness and reminded me that we will all be together again and it's only a temporary separation. It was especially comforting to know that we can continue God's work in Heaven.

Another night the Blessed Mother came to me saying, "Our Father has requested this experience for you. I am going to show you something." It was November 29th, 2013, a night

I'll always remember. The next thing I knew, my soul was out of my body and with the Blessed Mother in a dark, descending elevator. I asked the Blessed Mother, "We are going to Hell, aren't we my Mother?" She didn't answer. Finally the elevator stopped and the doors opened. I had no idea where I was. The Blessed Mother and I stepped out of the elevator. That is when I felt a female presence behind me. I quickly turned to her and asked, "Are you of Jesus?" "We do not see it that way." she said; "We see it as, Jesus is with us," she simply said. I asked, thinking if she said 'yes', that would indicate to me that we were not in Hell. I now realized we were in the lowest level of Purgatory. As I walked with the Blessed Mother I heard souls crying out loudly about the many terrible sins they had committed on earth. They were in utter torment over the weight of their sins. This was a place of repentance, deep sorrow and atonement for sins.We came to a woman at a table, with a cuff on her wrist chained to a heavy metal ball. "Come here," she said. "Let me put this on your wrist so you can feel the weight of sin." She attached it to my wrist, and the weight was so massive, I felt as if I was being buried alive. The heaviness was unbearable and I pleaded with the Blessed Mother, "Please have her take this off!" The Blessed Mother looked at the woman, nodded her head and the woman released the cuff. I then begged her to allow me to see Midgie. "Yes, Our Father has permitted this," she replied. Instantly before my eyes was a bright light, out of which stepped Midgie. She was wearing a beautiful white dress and came running towards me saying, "I love you my friend!" She started hugging me, telling me how beautiful it was in their world. I knew my time with Midgie would be limited so I quickly asked her the first question that came to my mind. "What will I be doing now for God?" "Teach, Maureen, teach! This is what Our Father wants you to do now." At that instant, I heard Our Father. He said, "I must bring her back now." As I was still hugging her she vanished and only her dress remained. I felt her soul ascending and leaving. I then turned to our Blessed Mother and pleaded with her, "Please my mother, get me out of here!" Once again, the Blessed Mother said, "Our Father wanted you to experience this." Just then, my soul was back in my body. I was never so happy to see my bed. Overwhelmed by this experience, I called for Jesus, "Jesus, if I were to go out and tell people of this experience, it would not be good "PR" for Heaven! Just about everybody I know has committed a sin that was spoken of tonight!" Jesus then reassured me, in His confident voice, "All they have to say is, 'I am sorry', it is that simple!" After Jesus left, St. Michael came to confirm that I'd visited the lowest level of Purgatory. I asked Michael, "What did the woman mean when I asked her if she was of Jesus," and she replied, "We do not see it that way. We see it as Jesus is with us." St. Michael stated, "Jesus never abandons a soul." Jesus knew that they would eventually evolve and enter Heaven, so rather than cast them into eternal damnation (Hell), he gave them eternal life. The next morning, I was so unnerved by this experience, I called Mary Ann and asked her to have Fr. Whalen and Fr. Welch say some Masses for the souls in Purgatory and shared my horrifying experience the night before. "If only people knew, no one would ever want to go to this dark, perilous place. I have to teach people this! It is so much easier to correct ourselves here and repent, than wait until we're on the other side." I began to pray every night for the souls in Purgatory. I pray for their release into Heaven with Our Father, Jesus and the Blessed Mother. We can pray for them, and they can pray for us, but they cannot pray for themselves. We need to pray for their souls and leave the rest up to God.

Often, I find myself talking to the Blessed Mother throughout the day. I thank her for guiding me or just talk to her about the day's events. It gives me great comfort to know she is always listening and protecting me. One day I had just finished filling my pellet stove. My house was warm and cozy. I sat down and began watching the vibrant flame through the glass. I was reflecting on my disturbing trip to Purgatory. I began speaking to the Blessed Mother. "You have shown me Purgatory and then the lowest level of Purgatory but you have never shown me Heaven. Other people have had this beautiful experience. Will I be able to see it too?" There was no response, which was not unusual. Later as I drifted off to sleep the Blessed Mother showed me a vision of Heaven, a breathtaking landscape of beautiful green fields and iridescent blue mountains that continued as far as the eye could see. There were no boundaries such as time and space. The colors were so vibrant, unlike anything on earth. Every blade of grass was alive and infused with the serenity, tranquility and love of God. The light was brilliant. I had the feeling this Heavenly realm was much more of a reality than earth. I'm at a complete loss for words to describe the splendor and utter joy I felt in this place. I wanted to stay there forever and never come back. Our physical life here is but a flash in the pan in comparison to the eternity of Heaven. Heaven is forever and awaits all those who trust and have faith in God.

CHAPTER 20

"We are going to talk about life"

When Fr. Joe Whalen retired in 2014, I was directed by both him and Fr. Welch to continue on conducting the healing services and sitting with people. I was happy to accept, and I am currently conducting healing services once a month at my parish, along with other venues.

The format for the healing service is a short teaching given by me, followed by Benediction and confessions by the priest while I pray over people individually. Most of the time it will be my angel St.Michael who will dictate the words to me for the teaching the day before the service, as Heaven knows what this particular group needs to hear. I ask Jesus if there are any messages for each person. Many times, Jesus will say to me, "Continue on," indicating there is no specific word for that person. This doesn't mean that Jesus will not answer that person's prayer, as He hears and answers all our prayers, according to His will. He knows the soul; I do not. At other times, Jesus will give a message to the individual through me which could be telling someone about a past event, or a lack of forgiveness.

God will always reveal this in a very gentle way, so the person can understand the origin of their pain and let it go. God will always reassure that person that He is with them.

A woman who came to see me for the first time, told me later that she was very skeptical and wanted to see if I was a psychic or fortune teller. She said as she was waiting for me to pray over her, she was very nervous and kept praying to Jesus telling Him over and over that she loved Him. When I finally prayed over her I delivered the following message from Jesus, "Tell her I love her too!" She just about came off her chair! She received her confirmation.

I remember another night, a man had been praying silently to Jesus, "Jesus, I do not know if you have been hearing my prayers through the years. If you have, please speak through this woman and tell me." When it was his turn, I prayed over him and asked Jesus if he had any words for this man. Jesus said, "Tell him that I hear his prayers." The man was so grateful and thrilled to hear this.

On other occasions, a person will feel heat in their body or tingling. Heat is usually a sign of healing, whether emotional, spiritual or physical. Most messages are given to help the individual release their emotional pain so they can continue to progress spiritually.

If the message is longer, Jesus will often assign St. Michael to expound on the message. Sometimes I am just given the knowledge of what the person's problem is and I tell them that we will pray together to Jesus for this intention.

One day before one of our healing services, St. Michael told me that someone would be there who felt abandoned, lonely, and had no family. "This person feels they have no one." He continued..."Tell them the following. Heaven would like you to know, you have a mother. Her name is Mary. You have a father. His name is God. You have someone who loves and adores you. His name is Jesus. You are not alone; we are with you every minute of every day. Hold on to us and do not let go." I delivered this message to the group before the teaching that night. The angel (St. Michael) then gave me the talk for the evening. "Love for others is most important in our world. It bonds our world to your world. We ask for love and hope, that you hear us. It is our key, to our door, to our Heaven. Our prayer for all of our children is that they love. Open your heart, let others in and Heaven will be yours." After I delivered the message and the teaching I proceeded to pray over the people individually. One woman clasped my hand, gazed into my eyes tearfully and said, "I am the person the angel identified as feeling alone and abandoned. You will never know how much his words have touched my heart. God bless you!"

Here are a few more examples of the short yet powerful teachings St. Michael gave me that can greatly benefit us all.

"We are going to talk about life"
Life is a gift. It comes with hardship, pain and despair. However, if we have Jesus in our life, life can be joyful knowing we are not walking alone. Always, always be joyful for that is how we see and know Jesus. Let prayer be said that

we can follow in faith knowing Heaven will provide. We are one with Heaven if we accomplish this. Amen. Amen.

"Your walk with Jesus"
First step, know Him as your number ONE.

Second step, keep Him with you at all times.

Third step, Love as He loves.

Fourth step, Believe and trust He is walking with you in good times and in bad.

Final step, Care for others as Jesus cares for you with compassion, understanding, reaching out to help others with good intentions, and most important radiate love as He does with you.

"What would Jesus ask of me?"
Many have asked, if they could talk with Jesus, what would He ask of me?

1) Put self aside and service to others
2) Bring yourself down to zero and after doing so, let Jesus put a 1 in front of it
3) Be kind and patient with all
4) Always have good intentions
5) Always do what is in the best interest for the other person
6) Prayer, Peace, Love, Joy

This is Heaven's way, (that is how we get to Heaven)

"Follow Jesus"
If your desire is to follow Jesus and want to be of beauty, then you must master patience, love, compassion, kindness. You will find when you accomplish this you will lead a life uncommon.

"Heaven's definition of Beauty"

1) Patience with yourself and others
2) Love to all
3) Compassion for all
4) Kindness to all

"Forgiveness"
When we forgive, it's a matter of being at peace with oneself. Let go of your difficulties and follow Jesus. Forgive that person and forget about the details; carry on to better times. Let Our Father be the judge, for you will walk saying I am free. That is how we merit. It is best to let go of this on earth, as it is one step closer to Our Father when we pass. Pray for the grace to forgive; unforgiveness only hinders one's soul.

"To be Fruitful"
Joy is our word to you, love is our promise to you, peace will always be with you. Perhaps we should reflect... If you have Jesus you have joy, love is our Father, peace should always be within you. This is our way, our world.

"Security"
Our Father's hope is for all of His children to acknowledge Him and have security of knowing that Jesus will be there with them in times of need. Many do not see this. It is important to pray for a full understanding of this. It is also important to pray for our growth, love, faith and belief in Jesus.

"Words from Our Father"
Heaven is our gift to you, Heaven is our hope for you, yes, Heaven is our word. Why is Heaven our gift? Because Jesus died for us so we could be with Him in Heaven for eternal life. Our Father has hope that all of His children will be with Him, Our Father's word is His promise, and His promise is Heaven and eternal life.

I was invited to conduct a healing service at a parish quite a distance away. I prayed that day to God the Father. I asked, "Father, is this what you would like me to do?" There was a short pause, and then I heard His voice. He said, "No prayer is wasted. You will bear fruit."

CHAPTER 21

"Life with Me is Joyous"

I experienced years of torment by Satan and three years of training by Jesus and the Blessed Mother. It's been an incredible journey that still astounds me. The years of Satan's torment and then the three years of Jesus and His Blessed Mother training me for their service all prepared me for what I could never have done on my own. From my work with pediatric cancer victims, to alerting fortune tellers and my ongoing spiritual direction at healing services, it is so fulfilling to exercise the gifts God so generously gave me. My motivation continues to be helping people with their discernment, physical, spiritual, and emotional problems with God's guidance and that of St. Michael, and to bring people to the knowledge of and faith in God's love.

My intention is to bring all back to God, with the help of St. Michael the Archangel. I seek no recognition but only to serve and give glory to God and do His will. I have experienced many trials just like everyone else. I've been sick, I've been healthy. I've been poor, I've had wealth. I've been attached to material things; I've detached myself from worldly things. I've been disappointed, betrayed and suffered the loss of loved ones. I've battled with Satan, and I've had the great privilege of being in direct contact with Our Father, Jesus, the Blessed Mother and St. Michael the Archangel. When a person is sitting with me, I completely understand, empathize and relate to what they are experiencing and have full compassion for them. I believe God has permitted me to experience this wide array of human conditions to strengthen and enlighten me so I can serve His kingdom to the fullest.

I realize what God has asked of me is but a microscopic piece of His infinite plan. We all have different work here on earth, but we share one common goal. That is, finding God, helping others find God, loving and serving Him and being with Him in Heaven. I was told the purpose of this book was to show that God does exist and that He loves each one of us equally and unconditionally. Hopefully my story, in some small way, will help others to know God, and learn of His love by understanding more clearly Heaven's ways.

Through the years, I have heard some say they wished they had my gift of communicating with Heaven. Most people don't understand that I didn't receive this gift overnight. My training included lots of trials and struggles. With this gift comes many responsibilities and sacrifices. My greatest struggle was detaching from earthly things. I found it an enormous struggle to give up the material world. I even remembered asking Jesus at one point why he had healed my health issues, because it would have been so much easier for me to die! That is how hard the training was for me. I remember dreaming of living a regular care free life again. Jesus ever so patient, continued to give me encouragement. A good example of this is when He told me, "You will have to endure people's problems, a lot of people. I will give you the strength and ability to perform this task. Your future is beautiful. We want you to be of beauty, poise, character and laughter." I now know and understand that there is nothing more fulfilling here on earth than to do God's work and to serve others, and I am totally committed to Our Father. I could never return to my old life.

Some have asked why the demonic attacks lasted so long. I believe it was because I was unshakeable and totally absorbed in my work. God permitted these attacks until He got my attention and I found Jesus. The assaults of Satan continued until I had no fear. I still experience interference, as do we all, but not on the scale of those early years. God will not allow a difficulty without having a divine purpose for it. I was instructed by Jesus, through Fr. Aniello, to tell my story. In obedience, I've written this book. It has been crucial for me to be guided by a Catholic priest. One thing I've learned is that earth is a learning ground as we journey towards Heaven, and the more we master here in perfecting ourselves through God's love, the easier it will be for us when we die. God teaches us in individual ways. I hope readers of this book will apply what I have learned to their own lives. Pain and suffering are not a punishment but an opportunity for spiritual growth. God always brings a greater good from bad situations. If everybody could 'hear' and 'see' as I do, they would realize how important it is to work on bettering themselves. St. Michael taught me how to strive to accomplish this while living on earth.

St. Michael also taught me that we must work things out before we die. If we are harboring any grudges, we must resolve them here on earth. We must forgive all those who've hurt us and also forgive ourselves. We must dismiss all judgments, resentments, and envy. We must pray to God for the grace to forgive, repent and tell Him we are sorry. When I would ask specific questions, St. Michael would often tell me to simply trust. I've learned that when you have God, you do not need to have all the answers; you just need to trust and follow His Will. If we have God in our life we have everything! Jesus taught me when it comes to His world, "to have faith and dance beforehand." Once we come to know Jesus, He gives us the joy and gladness that only He can give. The world can never take this from us. We are not only glad for our great reward awaiting us in Heaven, but we come to experience this joy here on earth where only He can transform our lives. Through Him we come to know true peace, hope and love.

Jesus taught me to follow Him. "The longer you walk with Me the deeper your roots will grow," He said. This has taken years for me to grasp. Now that I've grown deeply in Jesus, I have no fear of illness, poverty, loneliness... no fear of anything! This is the first step toward perfect love in His world. He wants perfect love for all His children. How do we accomplish that? By growing in our love for Him we will have deep roots, so no matter which card we are dealt we will continue to walk with and trust in Him. When we fall He will catch us, and when we fly he will guide us. This is His prayer for us, that we grow to trust and love Him so we can have peace on earth and eternal life with Him.

When I sit with someone I have no idea how that soul will be moved, how a life will be changed or healed. I found that I can never comprehend the magnitude of Heaven's words when speaking to a person. I just continue on as an instrument to convey God's words of love to that particular soul. I will be steadfast with whatever God asks me to do, and hope that many will come to know God through my story of Him working through me.

I prayed to God the Father, Jesus and the Blessed Mother and asked if there was anything else they wanted included in this book. I was told to add one thing. They want people to see, 'The Power of One,' that is, how one person can make a difference. They used my friend Midgie as an example. She had a driving desire to create a center for children with cancer because of the loss of her son. Her dream became a reality and success. God can work through one committed person, and even bring good out of the tragic loss of a child. She wanted so much to do God's work and He sent the people she needed to complete the task. God showed me that when somebody has a strong desire, the 'power of one' can reach out and touch so many lives. I reflected on the words of the Blessed Mother. She had stressed to me the importance of staying small (humble) while being one of God's instruments.

We must try to master the lessons we learn everyday with love and gentleness. That is how we are to follow our journey in this life. Love and compassion are two of the most important things in getting to Heaven. I will continue to do God's will and follow what He is asking me to do, with great love.

Jesus summed it all up when He told me, "Lack of Me is what My children are suffering from. Laugh, love and live together as one with all. Life with Me is joyous, life without Me is not. Lead your life within Me forever, never lead a life without Me."

MIRACULOUS MEDAL

*This is the Miraculous Medal given to
me by the Blessed Mother.*

*(Inscription reads: "O' MARY CONCEIVED WITHOUT SIN
PRAY FOR US WHO HAVE RECOURSE TO THEE")*

In 1830, one of the apparitions approved by the Roman
Catholic Church occurred in the chapel of the Daughters
of Charity of St. Vincent de Paul, on Rue de Bac, Paris,
France. On November 27, Sr. Catherine had a vision
where she saw the Blessed Virgin Mary standing on a

globe with dazzling rays of light streaming from her fingers and she heard her say: "These are the symbols of grace I shed upon those who ask for them." Around the Blessed Virgin in an oval shape, were written the words: 'O Mary conceived without sin, pray for us who have recourse to Thee'. Then she said: "Have a medal struck upon this model. All those who wear it, when it is blessed, will receive great graces especially if they wear it around the neck. Those who repeat this prayer with devotion will be under the protection of the Mother of God. Graces will be abundantly bestowed upon those who have confidence." The oval shape then turned around. She saw on the back of it the letter 'M', surmounted by a cross. Under the letter "M" (for Mary) were the Holy Hearts of Jesus Christ and of His Mother Mary. The first heart was surrounded by a crown of thorns and the second heart pierced by a sword. On the outer edge of the oval were 12 stars. In 1832, the first medals were struck and distributed in Paris. This medal from Heaven was at first called the Medal of the Immaculate Conception, but began to be known as the Miraculous Medal due to the thousands of miracles, healings, conversions, and protection attributed to the Blessed Virgin Mary's intercession for all those who wore it in good faith. Sr. Catherine became Saint Catherine of Laboure in 1947. The medal has the date of November 27, 1830 which is the date of the apparition where Our Lady presented the medal to St. Catherine. Millions of Miraculous Medals have been distributed worldwide. Many blessings and miracles have been received through this simple devotion to the Blessed Mother.

Maureen with Our Lady of Grace statue

Maureen and her Mom 2019

Made in the USA
Middletown, DE
29 June 2020

11499669R00149